Tweaked

A Crystal Meth Memoir

PATRICK MOORE

KENSINGTON BOOKS
http://www.kensingtonbooks.com

The names and identifying characteristics of some of the people portrayed in this book, particularly those in Twelve-Step programs, have been changed to protect their anonymity. In some cases, locations and dates have also been changed to protect their privacy.

KENSINGTON BOOKS are published by

Kensington Publishing Corp.
850 Third Avenue
New York, NY 10022

ISBN 0-7582-1265-8

First Kensington Trade Paperback Printing: June 2006
10 9 8 7 6 5 4 3 2 1

Printed in the United States of America

For Zelma

Acknowledgments

With thanks to Michael Bourret, Damian Jack, Ginny Lubbin, Sarah Schulman, John Scognamiglio, Kathy Watt, John Wise and, most especially, Joaquin Navarro, for their support and guidance.

Chapter 1

ZELMA

We can always gauge Tony's sobriety by his eyebrows. If he's been sober for a while, his eyebrows look a bit strange, too thin, and the skin surrounding them cracked, but they could pass for normal. If he's using crystal meth, the brows thin day by day, extracted as part of an obsessive project. He's unable to say just why he takes off his eyebrows but explanation is, frankly, unnecessary. We understand.

Today Tony is wild-eyed and his forehead is plucked as clean as a chicken's ass. Just two scabby rectangles remain perched above his eyes. He looks permanently startled and his face, fleshy to start with, is masklike, unmoored. He doesn't own up to the fact that he's been using, but his face says it all.

Obsessive plucking used to be Tony's exclusive province. As a drag queen once drawled when she saw Tony for the first time, "Well, honey, ya gotta have a gimmick." Now, however, Angie has joined the group and, disconcertingly, become Tony's best friend. The two of them look like off-duty clowns. Something's just not right.

Angie's thing is eyelashes. Less visually disturbing but, if you think about it, enough to give you nightmares, Angie has removed her eyelashes. One by one, she has tweezed them out because she believed that they were antennas broadcasting her location to the D.E.A. Even after she removes the lashes, they still have the ability to transmit information so each hair must be examined carefully, rinsed in rubbing alcohol to eliminate any physical remains linking them to Angie's body, and then burned. On her first day sober, Angie related this process to the group, as a kind of public service, sure that many of us also suffered from the same surveillance concerns.

Angie goes exclusively to gay Crystal Meth Anonymous meetings because she says she feels safe here. "You queens get me," she says, tears in her lashless eyes, whenever she shares. "We're all just tweakers here."

The world of crystal is filled with strange words and we addicts simply use them without question. I don't know why crystal is called tweak and I don't care. The sound of "tweak," like a stretched rubber band being snapped, just makes sense. Crystal has many names. "Tina" is a twisted contraction of the scientific name amphetamine. Then there are more colorful monikers such as Bikers Coffee, Chicken Feed, Crank, Glass, Go-Fast, Ice, Stove Top, Trash, and Yellow Barn. To me, it was simply The End. Crystal completed, with amazing efficiency, a trajectory that had begun with alcohol, moved through psychedelics, and escalated into a whirlwind of pills and cocaine.

Angie used to be a cooker so we hold her in high regard even as we resent the fact that she made and sold the poison we lived for. In her little trailer outside Desert Hot Springs, Angie had performed the filthy alchemy that produces crystal from a twisted recipe: Sudafed pills, the iodine used to treat diseased horse hooves, and red phosphorus derived from the strike pads of thousands of matchbooks. These rare ingredients were transformed into a toxic brew with the catalytic agents of Coleman's gas, muriatic acid, acetone, Methanol, and Red Devil lye. Because each step of the process is combustible and Angie loves to smoke, it occurs to me that Angie may not have plucked out her eyelashes but burned them off when she blew up her trailer.

Whatever else they might be, Tony and Angie are tweakers. Today they sit wide-eyed in their plastic chairs facing the rest of the group. Angie doesn't look at Tony but absent-mindedly reaches for his hand, which he offers without resistance, their sweaty fingers intertwining in unity and comfort. Tony's leg has been jumping up and down relentlessly but it stills at Angie's touch.

The rest of the group looks like the rejects of a tawdry gay bar. However, there are always the exceptions, those who show up not expecting a gay meeting or because they just don't care. There are sometimes a couple of young Cholos who tend not to speak but sit to the side in their oversized white T-shirts, baggy shorts, and white knee socks. They rarely return after listening to our litany of tweak-fueled sexual perversions. Then there's the infamous Marlene who appears to be a befuddled grandmother with a nasty temper. Marlene has the ability to piss off nearly everyone, but Angie hates her particularly and refers to her as "a second-rate fag hag." No one is even sure if Marlene is an addict although she once announced she was "addicted to prescription eyeglasses." She's an equal opportunity leech who shows up at gay twelve-step meetings around Los Angeles and positions herself in front of the cookie table. Mostly, though, she sits in the back where she has plenty of room because she can't stand to be touched.

A young Asian queen raises his hand, sweating, and the secretary points to him. His eyes dart around for a moment before he starts, "Victor. Tweaker."

"Hi, Victor," we mumble as a group.

Victor doesn't look particularly insane other than the non-stop tapping of his toe on the floor but his voice sounds choked when he speaks, "I need to interrupt this meeting and tell you all that I understand the code."

Marlene snorts from the back of the room until Angie gives her a glare. Victor starts again, "You all think I don't understand the signals but I do. If you're going to call the cops, I suggest you just do it and get it over with because I will not . . . I will certainly not tolerate any secret codes."

Victor has apparently finished his share because he stands up and walks out of the room, brushing past Marlene who rustles like an over-sized hen, sputtering, "Excuse me. Please watch where you're going . . . my purse!"

There are moments when I suddenly realize that I'm a nice boy from Iowa who is entirely comfortable sitting in a room of freaks. Our common bond is more than just crystal meth. It is a mindset. What seems like unhappiness to other people is just another form of intensity to us. And we love intensity more than anything else. It's why crystal was the perfect drug for us.

Still, there is a disconnect until I build the fragile little thought bridge that allows me to connect my early life to my current strange existence. Then the two merge, making associations. Like now, looking at Tony, I can think of nothing but Zelma. She too removed her eyebrows but, unlike Tony's, they never grew back. She always drew them on with a brown pencil that left an orange afterglow.

I raise my hand.

"I always wondered why I was an addict. Didn't think there were any addicts or alcoholics in my family. My folks barely drink. But my grandmother's dying now . . . and she's one of us."

★ ★ ★

Zelma Cooper Bomar Brauer Moore. By the time I was born, Zelma had already acquired her full complement of names, each taken from a man she'd worn out. Her pen name was Zelma Bomar and I guess she settled on that because Jim Bomar was the strongest of her husbands; strong enough apparently to feel up my mother every time there was an opportunity; strong enough to come back to Zelma in dreams that she liked to recount to the family. But, eventually, Zelma had planted Jim in the ground along with all the others.

I don't know my real grandfather's name off the top of my head and only recently saw a picture of him. I could have asked my father about him but my grandfather seemed somehow better as an enigma. Somewhere along the line I'd heard that Grandpa Moore had thick white hair and had lain down drunk, in a ditch, to die midwinter. That story came from Zelma, however, and I later learned that he'd actually died of something mundane like tuberculosis.

A few weeks ago my father mailed me a photograph of Zelma and Grandpa Moore. Grandpa is standing on a dock holding an enormous fish that he has evidently just hauled out of the lake in the background. In the photo, he is dressed rather elegantly for someone handling a slimy Northern pike. Zelma is sitting in the background, not looking at my grandfather but gazing out at the water. Both of them could pass for movie stars with their casually chic clothes and lean figures. There's no indication that these handsome young people are insane or alcoholic. In fact, they look perfect.

Of Zelma's men, Grandfather Moore and Jim Bomar remained shadowy figures but I knew her last husband, Carl Brauer, very well. He was a whining little spit of a man whose favorite phrase was, "Not like it used to be." And, indeed, it wasn't.

Zelma had taken up with Carl during my childhood because she needed somebody to drive her, having refused to learn to drive in a town where it was essential. Addicts and alcoholics have a way of getting people to take care of them and, for many years, Zelma managed quite well in an old two-story house on Locust Street where people came to pay court in her kitchen. Zelma rarely went outside in her later years, certainly never into the grass where she lived in fear of the chiggers that bit her ankles in summer. She was quite a sprout, Zelma. Nearly six feet tall with "I Love Lucy" red hair that was worn bouffant until she and the rest of the world unfortunately rediscovered perms. Then her hair resembled mostly a dark red scouring pad. Not one to be afraid of colors in her wardrobe, Zelma flouted normal conventions by mixing purple, green, and orange into her signature look—polyester pants in a single bold color, topped by a paisley or floral blouse further adorned with large stains. As for accessories, Zelma favored anything in turquoise or Black Hills gold, reflecting her fascination with the Southwest. She carried that theme into her footwear and preferred Indian moccasins.

Zelma had a constant supply of neighborhood ladies with whom she would alternate friendship and outright war. A colorful bunch with names like Gert, Ethel, Hilda, and Donnabell, they were received in Zelma's kitchen if they were in her good graces or gossiped about if they were in disfavor. In summer, Zelma would occasionally retire to the closed-in front porch where she could better see the comings and goings of Cherokee, Iowa. But I always think of her in the kitchen. Her extremities tended to be cold so she would often sit at her kitchen table, the oven door open and her feet stuck inside to banish the chill. She usually had a glass of something in front of her, along with a napkin on which she would doodle with a ballpoint pen. When deep in thought or during a pause in the conversation, she would take a toothpick and run it along the crack in the top of her Formica table, dislodging years of grease and crumbs. Rather than being horrified by the gooey indictment of her homemaking abilities, she would breathe a long sigh as if one of her daily laxatives had performed its duty with spectacularly relieving results.

Zelma was "creative." She regularly appeared in the *Cherokee Daily News* alongside one of her oil paintings of landscapes she had never glimpsed in person. Her paintings represented, I guess, the world she would have liked to have seen had she ever gotten around to it. True, there'd been a trip or two with Jim Bomar to the Grand Canyon, a glimpse of the Rockies, and even a stay with her sister in Pasadena. But these places washed over Zelma, insubstantial, in the face of her overwhelming fascination with herself. Although Zelma began her creative career in painting (resulting in two solo shows at the Cherokee Museum and endless blue ribbons at the county fair), she considered herself, I think, a writer. No, more exactly, Zelma was a poet. Her voice was sometimes jaunty on a bright morning in May when she was watching her beloved robins building nests:

> *I wish I had a spoon,*
> *as tall as the sky.*
> *So I could taste the clouds,*
> *Merrily floating by.*

More often though, it was nostalgic and came flowing out of her on a cold winter afternoon when she'd had a little too much to drink. Over and over, she returned to what seemed to have been her only perfect moment. She had gotten off the school bus as a young girl, her father had been waving to her from the fields and her old dog, Shep, ran toward her, welcoming her home. She played this memory in her mind any time there was a pause in life. She also recounted it endlessly, heedless of the fact that we'd heard it thousands of times.

After a dalliance with decoupage plaques, drawings on paper plates, and disturbing little dolls made from dried apples, Zelma created her masterpiece, which brought together all of her talents into one object and resulted in something of a cottage industry. On a wistful, not too dark day, she had written a poem entitled, "Little Gray Old Biffy." *Biffy* was, apparently, the word in Zelmish for the outhouses once common to old farmhouses in Iowa. Far from being a hated memory, Zelma associated the biffy with all that was quaint and right with the world before, as Carl put it, "It ain't like it used to be." The biffy poem was so significant to her that Zelma decided to enshrine it. After typing out the poem on a clean sheet of paper, she drew a little biffy illustration next to the poem. Still, it wasn't finished. She enlisted my father to cut and burn a scalloped edge into a rectangular board. Onto this board, the embellished biffy poem was cemented under a thick layer of decoupage and a piece of twine added for hanging. The Biffy Plaque was born. Literally thousands of Biffy Plaques were produced and sold in the Midwest. No self-respecting bathroom in the area was complete without a Biffy Plaque as part of the "country" décor. On many a morning, Zelma could be heard on the local radio program, "Swap Shop," announcing, "Got another batch of Biffy Plaques all made up and ready to go."

I keep a Biffy Plaque proudly displayed in my bathroom and have read it so many times that I have memorized the poem.

LITTLE OLD GRAY BIFFY

In blistering sun and bitter cold,
Battered and gray, it was growing old.

It was not a mansion, not even a hall.
Just one small room, that was all.
A place to sit, with Sear's book on the wall,
Was all the furnishing I can recall.
With panties down, we'd sit and look
At the good old catalogue book.
Hours and hours, we'd idle away,
On many a hot and sultry day.
Spiders made themselves at home,
And wasps built their houses in the dome.
Flies buzzed in and out the door
While crickets hopped across the floor.
Kids that live in town are spiffy
But miss the joy of an outdoor biffy.
Winter would come with a snowy blast
And you bet we got our job done fast.
The frost upon that icy seat
Would leave our butt print round and neat.
After all these long, long years,
We remember the laughter, sometimes tears.
Entwined in the memory of a childhood day,
Is that little old biffy, weathered and gray.

Like most artists, Zelma fought her demons. Throughout her life she took the "nervous pills" that had been prescribed during a stay at the Nut Hut when I was five years old. Having been offered the choice between Iowa State University and the State Mental Health Institute, the wise founding fathers of Cherokee chose the Nut Hut, thinking that it represented a more secure future. It certainly seemed secure, complete with bars over the windows and a guard at the front door to keep the inmates locked away. The unkind children of Cherokee had nicknamed the mental hospital the Nut Hut and it became the town's landmark. Built of dark stone, the neo-Gothic building could have been the set for any number of horror movies. In a town where all the streets were straight, the Nut Hut sat up north of Cherokee on a long curving loop of road. The Nut Hut's isolation on the edge of town kept it mostly out of our minds but we were occasionally reminded of its dark presence. Zelma delighted in telling me that she had woken up one night, gone to the kitchen for a drink of water and seen a young man standing outside the window, his mouth hanging open, tapping the glass with a long butcher knife. But, really, it never caused much trouble and Zelma never seemed to remember that she too had been committed there.

Many things made Zelma nervous but the "nervous pills" never seemed to do much good. Until I was six, we lived right next door to Zelma and apparently I sometimes added to her nervousness. I had a tricycle with a plastic tiger's head mounted on the handlebars, and if I pulled a cord, the tiger would produce a shockingly loud "ROOAARRR." Wearing a plastic Batman head, I rode around and around Zelma's house roaring. Strangely, my dad told me one day that the tiger had broken and that we had to throw it away.

I made other missteps with my grandmother that added to her nervousness. She and I often walked up to the movie theater for a Saturday matinee, which always seemed to be Don Knotts in *The Ghost and Mr. Chicken*. One day after the movie some of the neighbor kids asked me to go with them for ice cream and Zelma was forced to walk home alone. I imagine her now, rejected, dejected, and crying, heading for her jar of "nervous pills." I didn't see her for a while after that.

The fact was that the "nervous pills" were Mellaril, a fairly serious anti-schizophrenic medication never to be taken with alcohol. But the juice glass on Zelma's sticky table held little else than alcohol. Zelma liked a beer for breakfast, a little schnapps in the afternoon and whiskey or vodka at night. Ever the innovator, Zelma also fermented Welch's grape juice in a large jug with a balloon stuck on top. She believed that when the balloon blew off the wine, it had reached its peak. And when she once ran out of mixer, she informed me that she had figured out how to make her own 7-Up from sugar and water.

But none of this really mattered to an already strange, increasingly plump little boy. Zelma was my best friend. To me, she seemed absolutely wonderful. We had a private world, invented by her entirely for me. Her games were not to be found in any book on childrearing. She would build an odd little bed out of toothpicks with one last toothpick laying on top of it. "That's the man," she would say solemnly. Then she would light a match and set fire to the tiny sculpture. Somehow her bony fingers had twisted the toothpicks into a spring. After it burned for a second, the spring would be released and "the man" was catapulted into the air. The process was endlessly fascinating to me and her table was often littered with scorched toothpicks by the time I went home.

Another of our favorite games was "Watercolor." Zelma would wet a washcloth in the grimy kitchen sink. One of us would close our eyes while the other thought of a color. The closed-eyed player would slowly begin to choose colors.

"Is it . . . pink?"

"Nope."

"Is it . . . yellow?"

"No."

"Is it . . . brown?"

"YES," the washcloth holder would shriek and throw the wet rag into the face of the guesser. I could not have been more delighted.

I also liked to explore Zelma's house and, in particular, her "button drawer." Zelma was an adequate seamstress and, in the cabinet housing her sewing machine was a drawer that seemed to hold the entire universe in the shape of glittering, mysterious buttons. I could sort the buttons for hours as Zelma sat in the kitchen holding forth with the neighbor ladies.

Although Zelma's house had two stories, she only lived downstairs and slept with whatever husband she had in the bedroom next to the kitchen. Very rarely, Zelma would take me up the stairs to the unused bedroom that had been built under the rafters. The room was strangely Spartan for a house filled with clutter. Our trips upstairs were usually to retrieve or store one of her paintings. After pulling an old canvas from under the bed, she would always sit on the faded blue satin bedspread and look wistfully toward a mirror on the wall.

"Pat, come sit here," she would say, pulling me next to her. "You know Jimmy Bomar came to me here one night after he died." I had heard this story many times and the fact that it gave me nightmares only increased my pleasure in hearing it again. It was always dead still in that bedroom but the silence seemed electric rather than peaceful.

Zelma and Jim Bomar had apparently slept upstairs in this bedroom until he had developed some kind of cancer that took him away to the Veterans Hospital in Sioux City.

"Now, your grandma's just a little bit strange," she would tell me without expecting me to protest. "I see things sometimes. And one night . . . heck, it must not a been more than a week after Jimmy Bomar died, I woke up in the middle of the night and there was a wind blowin' right through this here room." As if on cue, she would stand and look at the mirror. She would hold out her hand and I would stand too. "I woke up that night and there was Jimmy Bomar standin' right there in that mirror, Pat. He was wearin' his sailor uniform and he was clear as day. Right there." She would stare at the mirror for a second, shrug and murmur, "Oh shoot," before heading back downstairs.

There was one activity that surpassed all others when I went to Zelma's house. She had an ancient old encyclopedia set that, for some reason, included major excerpts of *Alice in Wonderland*. Even after I learned to read, I still asked Zelma to read it aloud to me. There were two favorite sections that I requested again and again, both of which make sense in retrospect. I adored Alice falling down the hole into the strange room with the cake and bottles that would change her size. "Eat me. Drink me," said the cake and bottles. And indeed, later, I would.

The Walrus and the Carpenter also fascinated me. There was the trippy language but, more than that, was the idea of these strange creatures walking and talking, the best of friends.

"The time has come," the Walrus said, "to talk of many things: Of shoes—and ships—and sealing wax—of cabbages—and kings—And why the sea is boiling hot—and whether pigs have wings."

Another meeting. A.A. now. Note to journal: Is it pathetic that I still need so many after ten years? I've started going to a lot of A.A. meetings because the tweakers are too intense sometimes. A.A. C.M.A., C.A., N.A., a jumble of letters but the same idea. Get honest, give up, clean up. I heard somebody say, "It doesn't matter whether you take your alcohol in liquid, pill or powder. Doesn't make a goddamn bit of difference if you drink it out of a glass, shoot it in your arm, swallow it in a pill or snort it up a straw. You're an alcoholic."

Whatever. A.A. is just less intense sometimes. It is, in fact, almost respectable, like belonging to a civic club. This meeting is in a church, the lights are low, and the room is quiet. These people seem well. Nobody needs to get up twenty times for more coffee, nobody taps their fingernail obsessively against a metal chair, and nobody has scabs to pick. There is the hush of serenity.

A young man, a boy really, sits in front of me. His scalp has been shorn so that the hair on his head is the same length as the stubble on his cheeks. On the back of his neck, tattooed in wedding script, is the word "fearless." He can't be more than twenty and I wonder what happened that would cause him to need to be fearless, or if, in reality, he really is. Now that I'm in my forties, I'm beginning to have the disagreeable experience of seeing people like this guy as being inconceivably young. It used to be that everyone seemed the same age to me. Lately I'm drawn more and more to youth. I want to touch his head and feel the rough stubble.

A pixie-like woman stands and begins to speak. Her name is Joan Marie. She has a blond bob, very tan skin, and a voice that belongs to either a young girl or a very, very old woman. "Honey, I love my life."

Every sentence starts with "honey." Joan Marie's got twenty-seven years of sobriety and must be well into her seventies but she's childlike. I want to sneer at her plastic surgery and her pink twin-set but instead I'm transfixed. She's got the magic. "Honey, this is it. There isn't anything more. Stop looking." There is a kind of light emanating from her, around her. I'm not really listening to her words anymore but just riding along on this vibration that rolls out of her. Joan Marie is going into the hospital tomorrow for cancer surgery. She's lost one friend to a terrible disease, a sister won't speak to her, and her son is still out there drinking. And yet she's happy. As Joan Marie recounts her long list of woes it is as if she is describing winning the lottery and marrying Prince Charming.

There are tears of joy rolling down her cheeks as I realize that she is, more or less, saying good-bye to the group before she goes off to die. "Honey, no matter what, I'm just fine."

Joan Marie is fine but the truth is that I'm not. It's been more than ten years since I've snorted a line of crystal or coke. A decade since I've had a martini or a Negroni. Ten long years in which I haven't thrown back a Fiorinal or a Valium. And in those ten years, there have been periods during which I knew complete joy. But now . . . I don't really know what I feel anymore. Sometimes I feel a kind of humming that I take to be happiness.

Periodically, throughout my sobriety, there have been moments of crisis that bring me to a new level of surrender. I wish I could say that I actively search out these periods of growth and manage them carefully but, instead, I just wake up one day and feel them coming on like a migraine. Despite working the twelve steps, going to meetings, having a sponsor and sponsees, they just come. These crises feel like a slow-moving wave—sometimes in the form of depression and at others a kind of uni-emotion mixing anxiety and anger that rolls over me. As with a fever, the episodes of pain and surrender in my sobriety have always passed. So I give myself to them and try to believe that there is something better on the other side.

Unlike C.M.A., things are slow and formal in A.A. We line up to thank the speaker after the meeting, and I join the procession toward Joan Marie at the front of the room. She takes her time, saying something to each person, knowing that she may never see some of these people again. I barely know her well enough to say hello but, when I reach the front of the line, she peers at me with her piercing blue eyes, reaches up to grab hold of my face with her little hands and says, "Oh, honey, don't worry. It'll be OK."

My eyes fill with tears as she holds my face. I don't argue with her or ask her what she means. I hear myself say, "How do you get through it?"

She pulls my face down to her own and gives me a soft kiss on the cheek before she whispers in my ear, "You just stay. There's no big lesson, honey. Just stay."

I know she's right. If I just wait and let this period pass over me, there will be moments of happiness again. But, for now, everything hurts.

Zelma was quite a cook at one time. Her "Sunshine Cookies" were a study in simplicity with crunchy golden edges, a buttery center, and a scratchy crust of sugar. Her goulash with homemade noodles was hearty and straightforward. But, in the haze of Mellaril and cheap whiskey, Zelma's cuisine came undone as she developed an unfortunate fascination with frozen food. She seemed to regard frozen food as another craft project and was determined to improve upon the form and flavor of the basic ingredients.

The level of culinary experimentation was always highest on Christmas Eve, which also happens to be my birthday. By the time of my seventeenth birthday, the Christmas Eve dinner had become a sordid affair starting with Velveeta cheese on crackers and bottles of Cold Duck "champagne" to cap off the festivities. That year, as I neared adulthood, my father and I had decided to get drunk at the V.F.W. before dinner. This was not a typical occurrence but I think we both welcomed a little father and son bonding made easier by alcohol. By the time we picked up my mother and drove to Zelma's house, we were an hour late for dinner. Zelma was well into the Cold Duck and a foul mood. She brightened, however, as she revealed her menu, debuting several new dishes that showcased her particular verve. As an appetizer, she had created a Jell-O salad. Jell-O salads are a longstanding tradition in Iowa. Called salad and served with the main course, they usually feature Cool Whip and are largely indistinguishable from dessert. Zelma's version featured lime Jell-O with green olives and cottage cheese. Perhaps because it was so shocking-looking or I was so drunk, its flavor wasn't as ghastly as its appearance.

We ate in silence except for when Carl struggled to squeeze past Zelma on his way to the garbage can to spit out the chewing tobacco he'd been nursing in his cheek. "That's just plain nasty, Carl," Zelma shrilled.

Carl shuffled back, mumbling, "Ain't like it used to be."

I noticed that Zelma had not been roasting her feet in the oven. This was because it was fully occupied and now she slammed open the door, stared in using a flashlight, and clapped her hands. "Oh, goody!" First, she withdrew a bubbling pizza, a frozen one that she had topped with fried hamburger and more Velveeta. It was a revolting and greasy thing but we all managed a piece.

A few minutes later, she pulled from the oven an enormous ceramic bowl and inverted it on a platter. Out plopped what appeared to be a crispy basketball.

"Breaded shrimp," Zelma chortled. "Well, come on, kids!"

She poked tentatively at the mass of breaded shrimp that she had pressed down into the bowl with such force that it had massed into an orb of astonishing density. Zelma tried to grab a tail and pull off a shrimp but there was absolutely no movement. Not to be deterred, Zelma pulled out her largest butcher knife and began carving the shrimp ball into slices. There was something about the pink and the brown, the oozing of the grease and the sound of her knife against the crust that sent me over the top. Without warning, I threw up all over myself.

I came out of a blackout sometime later and noted that the mood was anything but festive. This was usually Zelma's favorite part of the evening. She and Carl would each sit in their big recliners with the rest of us on the sofa, all facing the television, on top of which sat a dismal little silver foil tree. Presents that would have been tucked under the green limbs of a tree in a regular house were shoved under and around the television at Zelma's.

"Pat, you play Santy!"

Zelma had decreed long ago that I would be the one to distribute the presents, but my saintly mother decided she would take over the process that year as I was clearly too drunk. Zelma's nose wrinkled with displeasure that the tradition had changed. However, she was soon distracted, and ripping into her gifts without noting who had given them to her. This was also a yearly ritual that particularly irritated my mother, whose job it was to sort through the wrapping later, searching for gift tags, so that Zelma could write thank-you notes.

I proceeded through my usual socks and stuffed animals, which were a mainstay of Zelma's presents to me well into adulthood. There remained at the end a small box. Zelma had long ago finished her unwrapping and seemed unusually focused as she watched me open the present. Under the foil wrapping was a much-used little cardboard box. I opened it to discover it was stuffed with tissue. As I pulled out the tissue, I saw something that was . . . too real. My grandmother had given me her first wedding ring. Black Hills gold: Three impure ores—pinkish, pale green, and yellow—were wrapped around one another and shaped into tiny vines with clusters of grapes. It was tacky, like all Black Hills gold, but significant because this had been Zelma's wedding ring. It had survived her multiple marriages and had sat on her finger for all those years as I watched her hands paint and write. It was a good-bye gift and my childhood was over.

"What happened to the ring?"

My therapist is a big leather daddy named Bud, who had been Mr. International Leather a few years ago. He sits like a Buddha in his stripped-down office in Silverlake. He wears body-builder casual wear that covers his fat muscles but reveals their shape at the same time. As he reaches up to stroke his thick black moustache, I watch his shirt's cotton sleeve fall back to reveal the veiny, twisted sinews of his forearm, covered in fur.

"What ring?"

"Your grandmother's wedding ring. You're not wearing it now."

"Oh."

"Wanna tell me what happened to it?"

I have this problem. I can confess to anything but it doesn't affect me. I have the ability to tell the truth while, internally, making it feel like fiction. But this time, I feel genuinely ashamed.

"I lost it."

"Um," Bud knows he's hit pay dirt and he's willing to wait. "Where?"

"I don't . . . I was really loaded."

"I think you know where you lost it."

"When I was living in New York, I came home late . . . well, it was morning. I was taking a shower and noticed it was gone."

"Where had you been the night before?"

"Oh, I don't know. Probably some club."

"What kind of club?"

"I don't remember."

Bud has stopped stroking his face and now has hauled those big arms up over his head with a deep breath.

"You're not done with your grandmother. Tell her you lost her ring."

"I could go and see her. I might go to a conference in Michigan and I could . . ."

"No, it's a lot more than that."

Bud has two big sweat stains under his arms. I wonder whether they're from nervousness or just lack of antiperspirant. "So are you saying I shouldn't go see her?"

"Call her. That's a start."

"I don't get your point."

Bud leans forward in his chair. His eyes are black. "Let's consider the proposition that if you remain as angry and disconnected as you are now you will someday use again."

"So . . . I should go back."

"I don't know." Bud smiles, "Just try to connect to the world. To your past. Own it. You're a writer . . . write."

I hate that Bud has a solution. I decide to give whining one more try. "I just feel lost."

Bud isn't having it. He's trailing his fingers through the black hair on his arms, rocking a bit. "When lost, I take a long look around and then I walk until I find something. I never just stay where I am."

Every day I think about not writing, about never trying again and ending the torture. I hate how the long days stretch in front of me like an indictment of my failure. I've known from the time I was in high school that writing was the one thing that I was meant to do. I even remember the exact moment that I knew I was a writer. Sitting in English class, I was writing an essay on Virginia Woolf's *Orlando*. I put my pen to the paper that day, felt my head tip forward, and I was lost in a trance of images and words. I no longer thought in the way that I had always thought. I thought on an entirely different level. The pages filled themselves effortlessly and, when it was done, I knew it was good. Instinctively, I knew that I was a writer but, in retrospect, I had done everything I could to avoid it. My career choices look like fear or self-hatred or laziness but I think I just got lost.

I studied theater direction in college along with a small sampling of English literature classes. Arriving in New York after college, I took a series of seemingly unrelated jobs in the art world as a young adult. For ten years before I got sober and five years after, I drifted through jobs that probably seemed important to others but meant little to me. Occasionally I would write something, usually in a fit of remorse over what I had done the night before, and it would be published. But when faced with rejection, I would just give up, get high, and forget about my dreams. What I never did was apply myself. In short, I fucked up.

God, however, is insistent that I am to somehow be a writer and sends me little signs now and then. Once, unhappy again that my life seemed meaningless, I went to a tired fortune-teller on Santa Monica Boulevard. With her head wrapped in a sort of gypsy cloth it was easy to ridicule her, but then she looked me in the face and I tumbled into the well of her eyes. Her fingers greasy with moisturizing cream, she had grasped my hand and smoothed out my clenched fist. She said, without knowing a thing about me, "You're a writer and you'll never be happy until you write."

Five years into sobriety, I decided I would try, really try for the first time, to be a writer. Now my life consists of an odd accumulation of tiny checks derived from academic books, shrill Op-Ed pieces, and barely sold screenplays that are never produced. But it never added up to riches or fame, so I often consider it all a waste.

The afternoons are the worst because all I want to do is sleep. This afternoon there is a soft Santa Ana wind blowing, and from my window the palm trees are nodding slowly, knowingly. I pick up the phone and call Zelma's nursing home. How many months has it been, maybe even a year, since I've called her? Her little cards and letters, stuffed with poems and crayon drawings done on napkins, have stopped, as if the effort for her to send them and me to receive them was just too much.

Before it rings fully even once, the phone in Zelma's room is grabbed from its receiver and bangs up against some hard object. "Hellllll . . . oooo?" Her voice is hoarse and tired, yet so entirely still her own, driven by a crazy energy.

Put down the phone, I think. Don't start this up again. "Grandma, it's Patrick."

"Why Paaaaat, . . . bless your heart."

I'm looking at palm trees and she's looking at . . . what? Paper plates she's drawn flowers on and stuck to the wall of her room? A gray Iowa dusk? No, for the moment, she's looking at me as I must still appear in her mind, unchanged.

"Where are you?"

I honestly don't understand what she's asking. "I'm . . . at home, Grandma."

"You live in California or New York, Pat?"

"I live in California, Grandma. Remember the pictures I sent you?"

"It looks real pretty, Pat. Real pretty."

We sit on either side of a long silence as the phone line buzzes.

"California," Zelma says. "That's so far, Pat."

"Yeah, it is." The guilt of her last statement hits my gut and drives me on. "I lost your ring, Grandma. I'm sorry."

"What?"

"You know the ring you gave me, Grandma? I lost that."

"Oh, heck, that don't matter." She's rustling around now, in her bed or in a chair, propping herself up. There's the rustle of tissues being pulled from a box. "What ring?"

"Your Black Hills gold ring. Your wedding ring. The one you gave me. Remember?"

"That old thing? I gave you that?"

"Yeah, and I lost it, Grandma. I'm sorry."

"Pat . . . I ever tell you about Black Hills gold?" I'm about to lie and say no but she launches into the story anyway. "Old French miner name of Henry was lost out in those hills, run out of water, food and . . . " She goes silent now.

I wait, knowing the story. "Did he have a dream, Grandma?"

"Did for a fact. Dreamed about grapevines by a river. Those old vines wrappin' around . . ."

"And he found water, right? So that's why Black Hills gold always has grapes in the design."

"That's right, Pat."

"I lost yours, Grandma. Your ring. Sorry."

She doesn't hear me though. She just follows her mind.

"Paaaat? You still a writer?"

"Mmm-hmm."

"Good." The rustling sounds like a mouse settling down into a nest of newspaper shreds and stolen tissues. "Good, Pat. Promise me you won't ever stop writing."

My grandmother who lies in a bed, dreaming about beer and her old dog, Shep, my grandmother who has never read a word that I've written, my grandmother is asking me this. And I can't promise her.

"I love you, Grandma."

"And I love you."

She doesn't hear that I haven't promised because her mind
has already moved on, chewing on sad old memories. All she
knows is that it's time to hang up, so she does.

Chapter 2

THE HOUSE

Days aren't bad in sobriety but the nights are still terrible. My dreams are filled with violence and crying to such an extent that I wake up in the morning feeling beaten. Last night was Tuesday, migraine night. Just like Zelma and my father, I have migraines on a regular schedule. In New York, I'd developed a taste for my migraine medicine, Fiorinal, a powerful muscle relaxant, and took it as regularly as aspirin. For years into sobriety, I'd simply suffered in a darkened room once a week rather than risk taking medication again. Now I take a nonnarcotic medicine, Imitrex, which magically contracts the blood vessels in my brain and stops the throbbing intensity of the headache. Even though I don't feel high from the drug, I love the ritual of taking it. I chose the nasal spray version of Imitrex and I snort it as deeply as I can, just like crystal, wanting to get its full effect. It also reminds me of the drug by dripping down the back of my throat, leaving a dull medicinal taste thrillingly similar to tweak.

Last night, after snorting the medicine, my head was spinning and the thought of closing my eyes made me nauseated. I thought that reading might focus me but, as usual, I made the worst choice in bedtime literature. Maybe as a kind of talisman from my childhood when it represented escape, I've always kept *Alice in Wonderland* beside my bed. I don't read it in a normal way but simply open it randomly as one would a *Daily Reflections*.

With my head throbbing, I'd opened to the section where Alice bursts into tears, crying so much that she floods all of Wonderland, stranding the world's strange creatures on a little island.

> *"I wish I hadn't cried so much," said Alice, as she swam about, trying to find her way out. "I shall be punished for it now, I suppose, by being drowned in my own tears! That will be a queer thing, to be sure! However, everything is queer today."*

Mostly I swim around in my head, engaged in magical thinking, looking for signs in the weather, lighting candles, praying for this and that. Last night, after Alice and Imitrex, I swam around in a dream that continued, boring but somehow terrifying, for hours. Dragging myself from a flooded field where long, brushy fronds wrapped around my naked body, I found myself on a muddy island. The inhabitants of the island were repulsively sexy Griffins—hybrids of men and birds. They languished, too wet to fly, and it was somehow my fault because I'd cried too much once again. Their feathers were matted like hair on a man's sweaty thigh and they lay, panting slightly, weighted down. The Griffins chatted in a weary way, not about me, but I knew the resentment in their eyes was directed at me. I had no feathers but lay bare and embarrassed, knowing it was entirely my fault. The more they ignored me, the more I cried.

One Griffin looked at me, rolled his eyes, and, in a perfect Bette Davis impression chirped, "Do. Shut. Up."

The phone rings and it's Judy calling from a parking lot in West Hollywood where she's setting up a tent for a sober dance. Judy's got something like twenty years of sobriety and she's the kind of dyke that I feel can take care of me. There's something very comforting to me about lesbians, especially ones who have a soft butchness about them.

Judy runs the House—a recovery center for gay alcoholics and addicts, most of them tweakers lately. Judy has an odd voice, harsh but childlike, with singsong dips and rises. It barks through her cell phone, "Wanna throw something out to you. Two of my counselors quit and I need somebody to help me run morning group."

I don't ask any of the questions that come immediately to mind. *How can you hire someone with no training? Will I do it alone? Is it hard?*

"How much does it pay?"

"Twenty-five an hour. Goin' rate."

"That's good but . . . why me?"

"They need to talk about sex. They'll be able to do that with you."

"God knows."

"Did it all, didn't ya, honey?"

And I had. Crystal and, before it coke, had been about sex for me. I was always looking to lose control when it came to sex, and drugs could take me there. My white powders were a passport to all the kinky, dark places that fascinated me but that I couldn't even approach when sober. When I get high, I don't chat with friends or clean the house or write. I head to a bar by the river, along the docks, or in a deserted industrial zone. With a little crystal, things that are just a bit off seem exactly right, an ugly man is an object of worship, and brutality feels like love.

Judy's made her offer and now she wants to sew this up. "So?"

"I'll do it for a month . . . if I can write about it afterward."

"No problem. See you Monday."

The House sits at the outlet of a canyon road in Hollywood, far below the glamorous mansions above, hammered into the hilly bedrock to take advantage of sweeping vistas and fresh breezes. The views from the House, should one ever look out a window, are far less romantic. To the north and the west, cinderblock walls form an enclosure as solid and featureless as any prison courtyard. To the east is an elementary school that periodically discharges its students, screaming with glee, into a playground. The students are probably unaware of the shattered lives in residence across the street but, for the newly sober addicts, the happy youngsters are a constant reminder of dreams lost. Instead of staring at the cinderblock or confronting the children, the addicts often stand on the porch smoking, looking south to a gas station and a dull gray motel sitting next to the freeway entrance. Beyond lie only dismal apartment buildings from the '70s built in a vernacular peculiar to Los Angeles, mixing complete flatness, tropical flourishes, and Spanish details into a hideous blend somehow more depressing than any trailer park. Even the names of the buildings—The Aloha, The Sunset, Villa Bonita, The Beachcomber—summon up visions of half-filled Mai Tai glasses on a Formica table with cigarette butts floating in their lurid remains.

The people who live in these apartment buildings are "below-the-line" as they say in Hollywood, the people with mysterious job titles like Grip, Best Boy, and Second A.D. This canyon is also a place for those who have just arrived from somewhere else. There is a feeling, above all, of transience. The sense of movement is deepened by the fact that the boulevard leading into the canyon is wider than is typical of such a street, so traffic rushes by at all hours of the day, cars poking and prodding their way into parking spaces and horns blasting at those who dare to hesitate. The street is also a draw for tourists because it leads to the world famous HOLLY WOOD sign, constructed originally as an advertisement for a housing development called Hollywoodland. Japanese tourists, in particular, stand fearlessly in the center of traffic to be photographed with the Hollywood sign looming over them, providing the necessary evidence of their travels.

Hollywoodland itself still exists farther up the canyon, at the very base of the hills where the march of rental buildings and bungalow complexes yields to Spanish-style houses after one passes through a stone archway into a tiny village. The village remains charming, hidden, and cloyingly picturesque. Its center is a café, open only for breakfast and lunch, that features country print wallpaper and a potbelly stove. An old-fashioned grocery, a dry cleaner, and a real estate office complete the village.

There is an uneasy, nervous feeling to the canyon, which suited me well when I moved to Los Angeles from New York. Even in the blinding California sun, the canyon feels dark, cast into shadow by the steep hills and overgrown vegetation. Thick coatings of ivy and tangled vines have slowly engulfed the houses. What seems lush and tropical on first viewing later reveals itself to be suffocating. A spiritual vortex was discovered in the canyon in the '30s and a succession of covens, mystics, astrologers, and cults had set up shop here, drawn by the sinister web of energy stretching across the hills. I was more of a spiritual black hole than a seeker when I arrived in Los Angeles but I, too, was drawn to the canyon.

On the bulletin board outside the Hollywoodland Café, I'd seen an ad for a one-bedroom cottage nearby. Long ago, Los Angeles was filled with small bungalow complexes, each built around a central courtyard. Many have been torn down to make way for featureless apartment buildings but a few remain, usually consisting of six to ten cottages with separate front doors but shared side walls. To a New Yorker, the lush vegetation, the storybook façade, the interior washer/dryer, and the cheap rent had seemed idyllic. At least it had in the sunshine. That winter it rained in Los Angeles for three months straight, as if I had brought with me a terrible wrath that somehow agitated the atmosphere, releasing a flood of rain. What had been a charming space in the sun turned out to be a pitch-black hole in the rain. Although the cottage's living and dining rooms opened out onto a tiny, private walled garden, sunlight never penetrated more than a foot or two into the rooms. Even though I had many horrible memories of my apartment in New York, it seemed, compared with this box, like a sunlit aerie, complete with a doorman and sweeping views of the Empire State Building. And then there was the cold. I had expected to find tropical weather in Los Angeles and was shocked by the unique cold of desert nights in California. Because older houses are rarely insulated here, many having been built only as temporary housing, they rattle with a persistent chill.

When I'd moved in, the walls of the little interior garden

had been covered in vines that flowered with lush, exotic flowers. As my crystal use increased, I became obsessed with the vines, sure that they were overrun with insects and other crawling filth. In a scene straight out of *Mommie Dearest*, I'd spent a weekend hacking away at the vegetation until only dirty white stucco walls remained, covered in little star-shaped brown spots from where the vines had clutched the wall before I'd ripped them away. My face and arms were covered in scratches, leaking blood, as I'd hauled the evidence of my "project" out to the dumpster. Along the newly blank walls, I planted a few sad little shrubs with variegated yellow and green leaves. They promptly shriveled and died, sitting loosely in the dirt I'd worked so hard to fertilize.

Everyone in the area seemed a bit off, including me. An old Latina woman ran the bungalow complex, appearing occasionally to gossip and collect rent. She said that she worked for the owner—a young, mysterious gay man who lived in Europe. Her visits became longer and longer over the months until I began to avoid her. Everything about her was depressing. Her matted black hair was pushed down on a heavy face, which was further hidden behind huge owlish glasses. She nearly always seemed on the verge of tears and, after I began to avoid her in person, she started to call. One afternoon as the rain pounded down on the roof and I lay paralyzed with a hangover in bed, she called, weeping, and saying that she had to confess something. She knew that I had raised money for AIDS and that my lover in New York had died. The facts of my life somehow gave her permission to tell me that she did not work for the owner but that he was, in fact, her son who had died nearly a year earlier from AIDS. The complex was in limbo, essentially abandoned, but she continued to collect the rent checks and deposit them into an account from which the mortgage payments were automatically withdrawn.

This confession served only to make me avoid the woman even further, shying away from her keening phone calls and suggestions that she could set me up on dates with her dead son's friends. I'd already come to hate the place, especially the private walled garden. For those who've never tweaked, it's hard to understand the paranoid insanity that comes with using crystal. As my weekends began to extend until Monday or Tuesday and then commenced again on Thursday or Friday, the effects of crystal colored the entire week and my paranoia centered on the fragile garden doors that separated me from a world beyond that had become entirely threatening. I can never think of that little cottage without remembering my last time using.

Los Angeles is the wrong place to be a tweaker. Too much fucking sun. My latest, longest run is over and the shadows are slinking around the floor of my bedroom, whispering to one another, as I lay in bed shivering and sweating at the same time. All I want to do is sleep. I hate coming down. It's easier to just use more. The exhaustion washes over me but I'm still a long, long way from sleep. The shades are drawn and I have been to the bedroom door ten times at least to turn and return, check and recheck the lock. There is masking tape along the door and window frames but the L.A. sun still glows through the cracks like a fiery accusation.

Whispers and crashes from the other room. "So obvious," I mutter. If they're coming in, I'm going to watch them do it. I can't take this sneaking around anymore. I jerk open the sealed bedroom door, smacking the doorknob against the powdery plaster wall, and stride into the living room. "Ha!" I shout and hear my voice echo through the room. Now it's in the open. Let's just see.

There is an overpowering scent of cinnamon in the apartment. Something sour is starting to smell under the floorboards and I have responded with an assertive cleansing of the air by boiling cinnamon sticks on the stove as often as I have time. In addition, I've found a product that I can put into my vacuum cleaner bag that spews a cinnamon scent into the air as I clean. The cinnamon nearly masks the sickening, rotting sweetness but I draw in several long breaths and know, without doubt, that the offending odor is intensifying. Those floorboards will probably have to come up soon.

Two sets of French doors open off the living room onto an interior courtyard. That's where they'll come in. The doors are locked but they're fragile and that's a problem I should have recognized a long time ago. There is *no* possible way to secure flimsy little panels of wood and glass. I carefully check the motion sensors that are attached to each door, pointing into the courtyard. Fortunately, I went to the Spy Store on Sunset Boulevard last week to buy them and now they guard every possible point of entry. I'm ready to wait and watch.

The living room is mostly empty. A boom box and a stained old sofa are pushed against one wall as if something were about to be constructed using the remainder of the floor space. I notice that I'm naked in the middle of the empty room and it turns me on. Something hot about the vulnerability. I sit on the dirty floor and rub into it, liking the scratch of grit on my pale, pale skin. It occurs to me that I haven't pissed in about a day and I run my hand over my body, inspecting it. My skin's so white it looks transparent and I can see a big blue vein in my leg pulsing and pulsing. Sexy somehow. Fascinated with my leg, I start to slap it and the glow of my handprint makes me think about getting on the computer to do some chatting. But it's too far and I'm here and suddenly the room is cool instead of hot and, after sweating so much, I just lay down to rest for a minute because it's not real, no one is breaking in, and I'm safe.

My eyes pitch and roll behind their lids. I'm not sleeping but watching intricate patterns draw themselves on the inside of my eyelids. And then the siren pierces my ears. My eyes open so wide that it hurts. Without standing, I'm across the room and by the door, looking onto the patio and fumbling with the motion detector, trying to turn it off. It's blinking and screaming. The noise is like nothing I've ever heard, sharp and pointed, scraping across my eardrums. I'm in the kitchen suddenly rummaging through the drawers, hunting for the butcher knife and back to the door with the knife held in front of me. The motion sensor is howling louder and louder, demanding attention. I fumble with it as I grip the knife harder and then throw the sensor to the floor as hard as I can.

Silence. I tap on the glass with the blade. Look, fucker! Look!

Because everything's moving, it's hard to focus on one spot. I try to keep track of the trees, vines, and shadows but they're all quivering. So I focus on the tree. And there he is. Waiting for me. He looks. A pause now. Coming down out of the little tree. That's how he got over the wall. I knew I should've cut the last tree down because now I see his hand extending out of the leaves, reaching. I hold my breath and push the knife out in front of me. I quickly run the blade back and forth over the glass but he still comes. My brain separates. One half of me is watching a man's hand in a soft gray leather glove push out of the tree as he descends into the courtyard on his way to kill me. But then there's that other half of me; the part that holds on and hasn't ever allowed me to get entirely lost. That other half of me watches the sad, pointed face of a possum as it lowers itself from a branch and licks a perfect orange.

I look into the possum's eyes. He seems to shake his up-side down head at me as he chews the orange.

"Please, God, help me." I haven't said it out loud but I've said it.

The possum licks the orange again and drops it. His mouth doesn't move but he's talking to me, to both halves of me. He looks like he might cry as he says, "I'll help you. But this is the last time."

Actually . . . that was a lie. That last part. Well, obviously, possums don't talk but there's more. So much of what I say is a lie. I've been lying for so long, in so many subtle ways, that sometimes I don't know the truth. It's not that I even mean to lie. It's my nature as a tweaker.

If I were to tell you the truth about that last night it would be both more horrific and more mundane because the reality is that it wasn't so terribly different from a lot of other nights. But there's another problem with the truth for me and that's the damage that happened to my brain. Most of the time I stand outside of myself, watching my life like a hazy, distant movie. Not even what I am doing in this moment seems real to me. When I snorted those stinking, off-white worms of poison, made from Sudafed pills, iodine used to treat diseased horse hooves, Coleman gas, muriatic acid, acetone, methanol, and Red Devil lye, when those worms hit my brain, they gnawed at it, leaving pathways, empty sections and memories that I can never retrieve. So the truth is mutable for me even on those rare occasions when I wish to tell it. Years fold to-gether like origami with details hidden deep in the crevasses.

So forgive me if I lie, but here's my truth today. I've blacked out since my first drunk at fifteen and crystal was only the last of the pills and powders and syrupy liquids that made me forget what I'd done the night before and the night before that. I would have preferred my drinking and using to be glamorous and fun but, invariably, it was just sloppy. With alcohol, I had a nasty habit of puking at inopportune moments and even a few drinks would produce an excruciating hangover the next day. Onlookers would laugh at me, thinking that I was pretending to stagger, but it was never an act. Pills always seemed like a supporting act rather than the featured performer so I would take them in combination with booze, usually with unfortunate results such as falling down flights of stairs high on Quaaludes and vodka. There were a few substances that never interested me much—especially pot with its half-assed paranoia and junk food compulsions. And I was too prissy and scared to get involved with heroin.

Cocaine and crystal were much more to my liking. As I'm rather mellow, at least on the outside, I liked their ability to push me to extremes. The ritual of chopping the drugs into a fine powder (I always preferred a razor blade to a grinder) and laying it out into lines fascinated me. I would cut and recut the lines, make them thinner or fatter, curve them into intricate designs, and then sweep them back together for another, finer chopping. Cocaine, with its white purity, was more aesthetically pleasing but, by the time I found crystal, I was less interested in pretty lines than in getting as high as possible for as long as possible.

It is immediately apparent that many nasty things have gone into the making of crystal. It has a faintly sharp and sour odor rather than the neutral smell of coke. Its color is, at best, the yellowed white of old linens. Meth has a strange texture too—both chalky and chemically moist. When I would snort a few fat lines of coke, there would be a slow elevation that built steadily but slowly. With crystal, the drug smashed through

my nasal cavities and bored into my mind with almost me-
chanical force. There is nothing nuanced about a crystal high.

The reality of my last night using is that I was thirty-one
and still alive, unaccountably, after burying my lover, Dino, in
New York and running toward something I couldn't quite see
in Los Angeles. I sold or threw away everything I'd loved in
New York. Of the money Dino left me, there had been just
enough left after long nights drinking and snorting to buy a
shiny midnight blue Ford Explorer and head west. That car
was the only thing left unsullied by my years in New York
and it represented some hope for me. On that last night, I'd
been on a sad date after a long hangover. I no longer remember my date's name but I recall that he was the consequence
of another long night staggering through a series of bars with
temporary friends and I'd wanted one of his buddies but my
date was the best I could do. So I went on a date with him
the next night because I was lonely and, if I squinted my eyes,
I could make him into someone else.

Our evening had begun dramatically with a traffic acci-
dent. I wasn't drunk at the time. It would have been less em-
barrassing to be drunk actually. Instead I was just hungover,
nervous, and inattentive when I rammed my shiny new Ford
Explorer into the back of a VW bug driven by a large, black
lesbian. Naturally, I wasn't aware she was black or Sapphic when
I hit her. She was just in my way when the light changed. So,
while my strangely nonplussed date waited in the Explorer, I
rushed forward to her car, sure that I could fix things once
again.

Waving my insurance card, full of apologies, I tried not to
look at the crumpled back of her car. That was fairly easy because she was so enormous and angry when she emerged from
the tiny car. It was beyond comprehension how so much wo-

man had been packed into so little a car. Even stranger were the series of low moans and shrieks she spoke in and that left me shaking my head in frustration at her inability to speak English. I tried the few words I knew in Italian, Spanish and French but they only produced more of her little grunts. I threw up my hands finally and said, "Look, if you can't even speak English, how can you drive?"

She looked me up and down, hating every inch of me, and pulled a pad from her bag. On it she wrote, "I'm deaf, you asshole."

When my victim had finally pulled her shuddering VW away from the scene, my insurance papers in hand, I looked at my car. Not so bad, I'd thought. True, the bumper now hung at an angle to the front of the car but, again, if I squinted, I could hardly see any damage.

I remember drinking at a Japanese restaurant with my date but I can't imagine what because I hate both sake and beer. The rest of the dinner has been lost to brain-cleaning fluid but the next thing I remember is being alone and extremely, exhilaratingly drunk, as my truck flew up Vine. It was late by then, too late to anticipate a car pulling out of a parking lot. Even before I smashed into it, rubbing alongside with the sickening scream of metal against metal, I remember blaming the other driver. They didn't look. Not my fault. And I just kept going, faster and faster.

Out of another blackout and I'm at the bathhouse and in a room. I don't remember who I was with but I remember crystal and then hours and then nothing. Nothing but home, exhausted, and so far from sleep. The part that wasn't a lie before, as far as I know, was that I sat that morning, watching the sun come up, absolutely convinced that if I took my eyes off those French doors leading to the garden that a man would break in and stab me. It was worse than that, though, because there was another entire section of my brain that knew I had gone insane.

And the motion detector alarms did go off but there was no possum that spoke to me. There was a neighborhood cat that bristled and ran away even as I fumbled to turn off the alarm. The cat said nothing to me. But when I went back to my bed, sweating and shaking, I said that prayer that all addicts and alcoholics must eventually say. *Please help me.* I said it to Dino, to the man who had loved me and died. And I did hear a voice. And it did say, "I'll help you but this is the last time."

Later that last crazy morning, I'd walked down the canyon road toward the House. I'd originally planned to drive but then I looked at my car. There was a long rip running down the side of my shiny new Ford Explorer and I knew I'd ruined the last perfect thing I owned. I couldn't think about whether I'd killed someone the night before or whether police reports were, at that very moment, being circulated listing my license plate number. I briefly considered removing my license plates but then decided all of that would come later and just walked down the street.

I'd noticed the House before in an offhand way. There was frequent activity there, people milling about in front, bedraggled men emerging from taxis and dragging in duffel bags. But the traffic moved so quickly down the road that I'd never really had time to slow down and investigate, not that I would have. But that morning, still vividly awake, I'd phoned Alcoholics Anonymous Central Office in Los Angeles, steadied my voice so as not to betray my state of mind, and asked for a meeting. After the person who answered the phone found out where I lived and determined I was gay, he told me that there was a recovery house near me that offered meetings open to the public on Friday afternoons. As with everything when I was trying to get sober, it seemed like destiny.

I remember very little of that first meeting other than the absolute cold of the House, its dimness, and my pity for the residents, even though they probably had more sobriety than I did at that point. But I do remember sitting and crying in that dim room.

Another of my lies is that the meeting at the House was my first. I had in fact made a half-hearted attempt to get sober in New York nearly a year before when I went to a famous A.A. meeting held in a storefront on Perry Street in the Village. The room was painted a sickening pink and, like all of New York, crowded and full of distraction. I arrived late, spoke to no one and left as soon as soon as the group had finished reciting the Serenity Prayer at the end of the meeting. I attended various other meetings in New York, getting a week or two of sobriety and then, when Friday night arrived, heading off to the nearest bar and my dealer. I was terrified, lazy, and not yet out of options. In fact, moving to Los Angeles was one of those options. Having exercised it, I was stunned by the speed at which the degradations of New York reconstituted themselves in a sunnier setting with palm trees. That finally got my attention. There was no more running.

So, in a sense, I guess the meeting at the House that day was my first because I was ready to surrender. Although it never occurred to me to check in to the House—I thought I was too far up the ladder to take such an extreme step—it became the center of my sobriety. I went to the public meetings held there on Tuesday and Thursday nights and Friday afternoons. It is hard to say why the House was so important to me. I would not meet Judy for several years and the residents changed too frequently to form friendships. Yet, for some reason, I felt utterly safe at the House. It acted as a kind of talisman for me.

As my world of sobriety expanded beyond the House, it all seemed like a great adventure. My cravings for drugs and alcohol had been miraculously removed and I was presented with a constantly changing array of friends, locations, drama, and revelations. I'd soon formed a toxic little clique of fellow newcomers and we went everywhere together. We had breakfast, lunch, and dinner together. Went to meetings together. Went to movies together. Fought and gossiped. I was no longer alone.

Los Angeles itself was fascinating because the meetings in each area had a different character. Because Crystal Meth Anonymous didn't exist in those days, I went mostly to A.A. with a sprinkling of Cocaine Anonymous. Meetings in the Palisades were filled with celebrity sightings and a mournful seriousness. Santa Monica and Venice meetings buzzed with hot young straight alcoholics as well as burned-out former hippies transformed into movie producers. Housewives in furs and diamonds populated Beverly Hills A.A. Silverlake and Los Feliz mixed leather men with artists and writers. And West Hollywood meetings were filled with show biz queens who knew how to put on a show.

I loved it all. Whereas going to meetings in New York had been depressing, Los Angeles was a huge treasure hunt.

Today the long gash in my truck is repaired, as if it never happened. But, as I walk into the House, memories of that first time walking through the front door flood back. Maybe it's the fact that Los Angeles is once again in the midst of a rainy winter and water rushes off the roof's steep inclines, gushing out of gutter pipes as if the entire structure is having a good weep. My umbrella is useless and I'm more or less soaked by the time I hurry through the front door.

A wealthy family must have built the House, maybe in the '20s. The entry hall is lined with rich wood paneling and a grand staircase angles around a corner of the room. A large dining room opens up to the left, in the middle of which sits a long folding table where a desolate little girl with ragged bleached hair is seated, writing in her journal. I see her from the side and know immediately that she's a tweaker. The muscles around her jaw look like steel cables moving under her skin, clenching and working away. I can almost hear the dull heaving of her molars as they grind against one another. My tongue moves over the roughness of my teeth, buckled and crumbling from my own years of gnashing away while I was high. Well into sobriety, I'd wake up in the morning, open my mouth, and my jaws would emit an audible click. All day long they would ache with the exertion of the previous night. Although I wear a night guard now that looks like a delicate version of a boxer's rubber mouth guard, my teeth are still tender some mornings.

The little girl senses me and her back stiffens. She refuses to turn around immediately but, after a long pause, casually pushing back heavy chunks of yellow white hair to reveal black roots, she looks up at me with eyes both hungry and afraid. She holds my gaze intently but, as soon as I smile, she returns to her journal.

On the other side of the entry hall is the living room, which functions as the public part of the House. This is the same room where I used to sit and weep on rainy Friday afternoons ten years before. A U-shaped configuration of sofas is already filled with residents who are reading from *Twelve Steps and Twelve Traditions*. A man with long, soft brown hair, drawn up into a bun on top of his head rocks back and forth, reading aloud slowly with the aid of an enormous magnifying glass, "Until he humbles himself, his sobriety, if any, will be pre . . . pre . . ."

From somewhere else in the room, a voice rings out, "Precarious."

The man who is reading looks up. His eyes are entirely opaque but they ring with anger, "I know what it says." He returns to the page. "Precarious. I know what it says. Of real happiness he will find none at all."

"You know Ding-Dong?" I jump and see Judy standing next to me, smiling.

"Ding-Dong?"

She juts her head toward the room. "That's what they call him. Walks around swingin' his head like a bell. Sweet guy. Doin' really good."

I follow Judy into the office. It must have been the original kitchen but, since then, a larger restaurant-style kitchen has been built on. The room now contains a mass of papers, pill bottles, and donated clothes stacked onto four desks. Judy swings open a refrigerator and grabs a Diet Coke from between more bottles of medicine.

Judy reminds me of a pro-golfer. She's wearing sensible slacks, a sporty sweater and sneakers. Her sandy hair is cropped boyishly short and she looks as if she should be coaching women's track at some midwestern university. Instead, she lives in Los Angeles surrounded by tweakers, storms of emotion breaking over her every day. Called behind her back both Mother and Mr. Judy by the residents, she's much hated by those who don't make it through the program. In fact, she and her partner, a sweet Latina who also works at the House, have been in a kind of hiding for the past few months. A former resident, now using crystal again, regularly calls to inform them that he knows where they live and is preparing to kill them. This they could bear and had, in fact, experienced several times before. Now, however, they have a child and the equation has changed. Judy recently came across a website created by the stalker, complete with a photo of their child and plans to kill the boy. Judy and her partner fled north with their son for a few weeks when it became clear that the local police would provide little protection unless the stalker had actually attacked them. They've since returned to the city but now have personal security, paid for by Judy's mother.

Judy just stands there, swigging her Diet Coke, seemingly unconcerned that her stalker could be circling outside, having grown accustomed to yet another strangeness in life. Most of Judy's life is strange, which is another way to say that it is miraculous. Twenty years ago she was a resident in the House, having burned out her parents and her options while chasing drugs and alcohol. After having completed the program, she worked to get certified as a drug counselor and returned to eventually become the director. Because she's an alum of the House, she carries an undeniable level of authenticity when she lowers her head and bellows at the newest resident, "Stop the fuckin' lies, queen!"

There's something about Judy that completely reassures me that she knows what she's doing. I feel cradled by her authority.

"We've got a bunch in here, let me tell ya."

"I'm kinda nervous." This is only partly the truth. In reality, I feel completely exhilarated. "Excited too."

"So you'll just run the morning rap group. You won't have to get all involved with the paperwork."

"I don't know what to do . . ."

"You'll learn real fast. The main thing is they need to talk about sex. That's what takes 'em out mostly. They can have whatever kind of sex they want. It's not about right and wrong. I just want 'em to do it without killing themselves."

"Or each other."

"Exactly."

"So . . . why me? I'm not trained at this."

"You need a job, right?"

"Well, I've got some projects I'm working on . . ."

Judy's gaze doesn't flicker. "Right, but I mean a job where you get paid . . . regularly."

I immediately feel defensive. "Well, there's getting paid and getting paid enough to pay the rent."

"So this doesn't have to be forever if something else comes along. In the meantime, you know how to talk about sex, we get along and I think you'd do a good job. Work for you?"

There are those moments when I know I'm getting what I need rather than what I want and this is one of them. I hear myself say, "Works for me. Thanks."

"Great!" Judy finishes off her Diet Coke, scores a perfect basket with the can and says, "Ready to get started?"

Chapter 3

GROUP

Most of the residents do not look up as I walk in with Judy
but I can feel the waves of tension roll across the old brown
carpet. I hear someone whisper, "Mother," but Judy, if she
hears it, just sits down. Sofas line the long walls of the room,
facing in against one another. Judy and I sit in chairs that
form the bottom of the U-shaped configuration. At the other
end of the room, logs crackle in the fireplace in a vain attempt to bring some warmth to the damp old walls.

"This is Patrick. He's going to be helping in Group."

The residents nod. They're an assortment of castoffs. The
gay community always strives for diversity but it is seldom
seen except in rehabs and hospitals. This room is an amalgam
of constituencies that progressive groups can only dream of
reaching. Half the faces are black or brown. The ages range
from twenties to sixties. But now that I look more closely, I
realize that the room is not diverse at all. As wide as the spec-
trum might be, the group is still comprised mostly of gay men.
An obviously transgendered woman stares out at me from
behind fishbowl glasses. There is only one very broken down
older dyke, folded deep into the recesses of a sofa, her arms

wrapped around a tattered pillow with a needlepoint image of a leaping dolphin. She hugs it like a shield. And in a city of Koreans, Thais, Japanese, and Chinese, there are no Asian faces.

Conversation stops as Judy peruses an attendance list. Finally, she looks up and focuses on a rail thin black man. Lewis. He looks like a black skeleton to me. The flesh of his cheeks have been eaten away by HIV meds, his jaw is overly pronounced, and a ring of fat has swollen his neck in a syndrome called lipodystrophy or, on the street, "puppet face."

"So, Lewis." Judy's voice is like a can opener. Lewis's body has been rigid but, at the sound of her voice, his hands flutter loose from his lap to straighten his sweater and then pick at his head.

"Yes." His voice nearly cracks with strain.

"Why you so nervous? What's up with you?"

"Up?" He wraps his legs tightly around each other.

"Yeah. You look like you're gonna explode. What's up?"

Lewis carefully shuts down his emotions and straightens his body. "I don't know what you mean Judy. I'm doing real good. I've been sharin' my feelings with my peers and . . ."

"Queeeeen," Judy's voice is so sharp and loud that I pull myself up in the chair. "I hear you called your parents yesterday."

Lewis looks down now, preparing. He mumbles, "I needed them to drop off some of my papers and . . ."

"Stop lying!" I glance at Judy, eager to see the face that could go along with such a voice. I expect to see a red face, eyes bugged out, and fists clenched. Instead, she looks relaxed, almost smiling. "You needed them to drop off some fancy new clothes for you to fix your feelings."

Lewis's head comes up now at the prospects of Judy messing with his wardrobe. "Those were my clothes."

"You buy 'em?"

"I sure did." His eyes are wide now.

"Yeah, with mommy's credit card."

"I never asked them for nothin'. They always wanted . . ."

"Shut the fuck up, queen. You're lying." Lewis returns his gaze to the floor, regrouping. "What's the rule about not contacting your family or your spouse for thirty days?"

"I needed some . . ."

"What?" There's a vibration in the room that comes both from energy bouncing off the walls and the reverberation of Judy's voice. "What's the rule, Lewis?"

"But I needed clothes. How I'm supposed to be without wardrobe?"

"Are you naked, queen? Anybody seen Lewis walk around here naked?"

Another black queen, big and muscular, drawls out, "He didn't have no Ralph Lauren. That's the problem."

Lewis draws up, attacked from both sides. "I didn't ask them to bring me nothin' new. Those sweaters are old."

The other queen can smell blood. "Well, they had Macy's tags on 'em."

"What's the rule, Lewis?" Judy screams.

Lewis, sensing that the battle is over now that Judy has a collaborator, withdraws completely, his arms folding over one another. Judy's voice softens, "Honey, the problem is that no matter how many sweaters your mom buys you at Macy's, you're still gonna be a bottomed-out tweaker in a recovery house. Let me ask you something."

Lewis focuses on a dust ball that peeks out from under the long coffee table in the middle of the room. "Lewis!" Lewis looks up reluctantly. "You always had nice clothes? You ever wear trash?"

Lewis knows it's a trap but he can't resist. "I always had nice clothes."

Judy's voice is soft now, modulated. "And you still never felt right, I bet. You always felt like a piece of shit no matter how nice those clothes were. Am I right?" Lewis nods warily. Judy gestures to the room. "Like all of us. No matter how nice that . . . .stuff . . . was. Never fixed us. None of us. We never felt like we belonged. Never felt comfortable. Most of us since we were kids. Like we were from another planet. No matter how much shit you got, nothin's ever going to fix your feelings, Lewis."

There is a flicker of recognition in his eyes but then Lewis looks back at the floor and says flatly, "Those are my clothes and I don't see nothing wrong with havin' nice things."

Lewis doesn't break. For two hours, Judy focuses her jack-hammer of a voice on him and, if anything, he seems to withdraw further and further. My head is pounding and I feel faint but Judy's energy never wavers. With Group coming to a close, Judy says, "Lewis, how does it feel to be so unwilling that some fuckin' sweaters are more important than saving your life?" He just glares. "One more chance, Lewis. Use your feelings list."

Lewis opens his list slowly, deliberately. I have one lying open in my lap and my eyes scan the list of emotions he might pick. Angry. Depressed. Disturbed. Fucked up. Sweaty. Wicked. Lewis stares at the list for a moment and licks his lips that look like strips of dry rubber stretched across his bony face. Slowly, deliberately, he rips the list in half, throws it in the fireplace and, hand on hip, walks out of the room.

As Lewis passes Judy, he snaps his fingers and sneers, "Bye, bye, sweetheart."

Judy just sings out, "Bye, honey," as we watch the feelings list smolder in the fireplace. "Don't forget all those pretty sweaters upstairs. Those'll keep you sober."

The residents, usually near sleep, are sitting ramrod straight on the sofas, staring at Judy. She sucks at something stuck in her teeth and crosses her legs. She smiles and trills, "It's not over. Just wait."

We sit silently and I find myself counting in my head, *One, two, three*. I hear a door slamming over and over again as if Lewis is trying to beat a doorframe into submission. Judy tips her head back and her voice slices through the ceiling, "You break a door and we'll call the police."

Silence and I start again, *Four, five, six*. Lewis is on his way down the stairs now, making a rumble that is totally out of proportion to his skinny frame. He's in the doorway now, his chest heaving and eyes wide. His voice is screeching like a crow as he points his finger at Judy, "I waaaant everything, I mean every single fuckin' thing I came in here with."

Judy doesn't bother to stand up but shouts, "You came in here pushing a shopping cart, queen! It's still out by the garage. Get it out of here!"

Lewis half-dances across the room, a demented marionette, flinging a chair and kicking the coffee table as hard as he can. One of his eyelids is drooping now and his face is contorted as he screams at Judy, "You fuckin' bitch whore dyke."

"Ooooh, I'm a dyke. I didn't know! What else ya got for me?"

"And your girlfriend's a dirty Mexican whoooore!" Lewis grabs a pillow from the sofa and flings it as hard as he can at Judy. Without seeming to move, Judy is on her feet, has caught the pillow, and is shoving Lewis out of the room.

There are unintelligible shrieks coming from Lewis now as he backs toward the front door, crouched down. He starts to walk back toward Judy and a couple of the bigger male residents take up position around her. Lewis turns on his heel, heads out the front door, and slams it behind him with such force that the glass shatters. It doesn't rain down on the floor but, with a tinkling sound, cracks with a thousand little lines.

After Group, I came home, curled up in my cool, quiet bed, and cried.

My feelings had less to do with Lewis than seeing the power of addiction. It's been in my face lately. Last night, I went to a crystal meth meeting and saw Sam. I never really knew much about Sam except that he would stand up every few weeks as a newcomer. He was a sweet guy, not too crazy, but not making any progress either. The meeting was nearly over last night when the door slammed open and Sam jerked through it, his limbs jumping as if he were being shocked. There were sores all over him and he was dirty enough to stink.

Sam made a beeline for the empty chair next to me, flung himself into it, and began to sob. For the past few years, I've gotten in the habit of keeping my distance in meetings but there was something about Sam that wasn't frightening, just overwhelmingly sad. The meeting continued on, as they do, despite Sam's sobbing. When I put my arm around him, he leaned his head on my shoulder and cried as I stroked his filthy hair.

I took Sam out of the room and bought him something to eat. He mostly couldn't talk, just cry as his muscles jumped involuntarily. There was a hospital bracelet around his wrist and I asked him why he'd been admitted. He gulped, "Overdose," and tried to eat, splattering the soup across the table. He looked at me wildly and said the words I dread, "Please help me. I don't wanna be on the streets."

"Sam, you're high, right?"

He shook his head, too weak to even really lie.

"You can't stay with me, Sam. I'm gonna take you to another meeting and you need to make an announcement, ask for a place to stay."

A few minutes later I put Sam in a seat at a late night meeting, still jumping, and trying to hold onto the soda I'd bought for him. He cried and put his arms around me again. "Please, I can't be on the street again." And then I left.

I cried all the way home for him and for me. It's not that I know Sam and it's not that I would even consider letting someone who's high into my house. It's just that for the first time, in a long time, I find I can't keep my distance from this disease and I wonder sometimes if I can take much more. Meetings are the medication for alcoholics and addicts but the side effect of that medication is the pain of seeing people dying, over and over again, relentlessly. I'm so worn down by death. It's true that there is the joy of seeing people live and recover, and knowing that I've lived too. But that joy is always tempered by knowing that most don't.

Somehow I thought, having survived AIDS, things would lighten up. But this is how my world has always been and, in many ways, I sought it out. As a child, long before I took my first drink or found drugs, I spent my days wrapped in lonely fantasies, drawn to everything dark and mysterious. When I moved to Pittsburgh, the ruined steel mills fascinated me more than the city's gleaming shops and museums. In New York, I was drawn instinctively to the deep shadows of the crumbling West Side Piers with their promise of danger. But in my late twenties what had been a youthful pose of artistic intensity became all too real as I watched people wither away in front of me, first from AIDS and then from addiction. Now I want the intensity to stop but it just goes on.

Now, late in the afternoon, I sit, groggy, flipping through

old photo albums. Here's a yellowed copy of the *Cherokee Courier* ("Published Daily, except Sunday, Wednesday, Friday, and Saturday.") from Thursday, December 22, 1966. I would have been two days short of four on that day. There are several enormous photos of me on the front page of the paper under the headline, "May Christmas Be a Magic Time of Happiness for You." I'm dressed in my finest pajamas with a pair of white gym socks peeking out from the pants. A Christmas tree, swirled in what was called "Angel Hair" but was probably made of asbestos, stands partly visible beside me. In the first photo, I smile out at the camera, rather dashing for an almost-four-year-old I think, holding an empty box. The caption reads, "Take a great big box, fill it full of Christmas cheer and happiness, trim with the glitter of hope . . ." In the next photo, I'm focused on wrapping the box as the words trail along below, "Wrap in gay paper and tie with bright ribbons, bows of red, silver and gold, fashioned by hands that care . . ." In the following pictures, I am nearly finished with my wrapping, and a large pile of presents has appeared behind me. "Add a generous sprinkle of love, a sunny smile, and a heart full of good wishes for the merriest and most joyous of Christmases . . ." And, finally, my package has been completed and I am standing, holding an enormous Christmas stocking with a greedy grin on my little face. "Pack the overflow in a boy's big red stocking and you'll begin to know how many good wishes we're sending your way this Christmas Time."

It was apparently an extremely slow news day because the lower half of the front-page also carried a story on me along with a smaller photo. I don't recognize the smiling boy from staged photographs on the upper page. This boy, however, I know. He looks into the middle-distance, eyes a bit glazed and staring intently at something other than the photographer. Perhaps I'm thinking of the significance of the headline to the right of my head, "5,856 Persons on Farms in This County" or am already stewing in jealousy that "Miss Sharon Hogan of 920 West Willow, Cherokee, is among the members of a choir who will be seen on a special holiday television program."Whatever I'm thinking, my eyes look like Zelma eyes; focused elsewhere.

The story next to my photo begins, "The handsome charmer illustrating our Christmas wishes is Patrick Wayne Moore, who stages a double celebration each Christmas season." I hear my mother's happy voice singing out "Happy Birthday, Christmas Baby!" Then Judy's voice echoes in my head, "We never felt like we belonged."

At about the time of this brief flash of celebrity at age four, I had my first drink. Not that the drink led to alcoholism or was even particularly inappropriate—my cousins also had little holiday drinks and never turned out to be raging drunks—but that Sloe Gin Fizz is forever etched in my memory as magical and inexplicably glamorous. Each year at Christmas, Sloe Gin Fizzes would be served to the children of our family as part of the festivities.They were dispensed in small metal glasses cast in varying jewel-tones. My glass (and it was absolutely *my* glass) was dark purple. It was not reflective but burnished with a slight texture that helped my tiny fist grip it tightly.The glass would frost on the outside in response to the cool liquid within.

Though I certainly didn't know it at four, sloe gin is actually made from a berry called a sloe, harvested from blackthorn hedges in October and deposited into a half empty container of gin along with a heaping cup of sugar.The resulting liquor is deceptively syrupy but retains the full potency of regular gin. A Sloe Gin Fizz, consisting of sloe gin and 7-Up over ice

and garnished with a red maraschino cherry, is a drink probably best enjoyed by those ten and under but, for me, it still
carries with it the memory of festivity and warmth, both of
which it produced in me for many Christmases to come.

My first true drunk was self-induced a decade later and
featured most of the elements of my subsequent drunks over
the next fifteen years. The cocktail that produced my first real
drunk was Triple-Sec on the rocks, a drink that Zelma would
have approved of for its sheer potency and sweetness. One of
my few friends in early high school came to my house and I
suggested we get drunk from the bottle that had been sitting
in my parents' refrigerator for the past three years. In the back
of my mind, I hoped that this might also lead to the end of
my virginity with this sweet boy who sang Simon and Gar-
funkel songs while playing his guitar. Rather, like most of my
drunks, it led to a display of my virtuosity at being an idiot
and thinking I was funny. In this case, I sat at the top of the
stairs and plopped down one at a time on my ass, laughing
hysterically. Later, I vomited and blacked out—also mainstays
of my repertoire.

Perhaps drugs were later so appealing to me because I
handled liquor so badly. Another feature of my Iowa drinking
life, which would reappear when I moved to Los Angeles, was
driving while blind drunk. Iowa had made a few half-hearted
attempts at discouraging drunk driving, mostly displays of grue-
some photographs at the State Fair. These photos attracted a
wide audience of groaning and giggling teenagers who loved
the gross-out factor of the decapitation photos; for some reason, many people in Iowa quite literally lose their heads while
drinking and driving. These displays, and the somber highway
patrolman who always stood alongside them, never dissuaded
me from getting behind the wheel loaded. The fact is that, in
Iowa, one has to drive to get anywhere. Taxis and buses were

still unknown luxuries of city life so there were very few alternatives to the point and shoot approach of drunk driving.

Fortunately for me there were few obstacles when my car shot off the road, which it did on a regular basis. My car would careen down into the ditch, smack up over a small hump and continue on into a cornfield. While cornfields do not make for a smooth ride, one can go for a surprisingly long distance over the furrowed ground, reach another road, and continue on without much fuss. My father regularly asked me about the grass and dirt sticking out from the underside of my bumper but I would simply look into the distance and shrug.

Drugs soon supplemented liquor and, together, they solved one of the largest problems of my adolescence—obesity. I'd been fat since I was five or six, tipping the scales at two hundred pounds by the time I reached Fifth Grade. It would be tempting to blame my weight on Iowa's cuisine, built on staples such as French onion dip and Tater Tots. But mostly my fat rolls were a direct reflection of sitting on the sofa and staring at the television as a bored and lonely little boy.

My weight problems disappeared in high school around the time I developed a small cadre of bad girls. These girls all tended to have enormous tits and wore their feathered hair blown back into huge cream horn curls on either side of their faces. Together, we would run through a full pack of Dexitrim diet pills most days in school. The very thought of eating became nauseating after a few surprisingly potent Dexis. Instead, we would sit in the school library, too wired to go to class, doodling maniacally in our notebooks and grinding our jaws. I dropped thirty pounds and, while not exactly popular, had found my niche.

My favorite of the bad girls was Staci. Staci favored skin-tight jeans, blue eye shadow, and signed her name with a heart dotting the final "i". She was particularly appealing because, unlike some of the other bad girls, she was not white trash. Her father was a lawyer and they lived on the outskirts of town in a semi-Swiss chalet. While my family had no Christmas tree other than Zelma's sad little tinsel number, Staci's family displayed a huge flocked tree, resplendent in its white coating and blue ornaments, in their perfect cathedral-ceiling living room. Staci always had two boyfriends—an acceptable jock from our high school and an older man from a nearby town. She never explained exactly how she found these men but there tended to be a new one every time she went to Sioux City shopping or to have her braces adjusted. I was often the cover for her overnight visits with these men in motels and my payment was a breathless description of their sexual explorations as well as the occasional joint that she had nabbed from one of her lovers.

I was a little in love with Staci, especially when she sang for me. Staci had dreams of being an opera singer but her repertoire was more Top Forty. When she got drunk and toked on a joint, she would talk about her latest boyfriend and how she was really in love with him but it would never work out. She would crack open another beer and become maudlin. "The Rose," starring Bette Midler as a Janis Joplinesque blues singer had opened in theaters the year before, and Staci would often sing me the theme song, complete with a thrilling ending where her voice would break and she would try to make-out with me even though I suspect she was pretty clear on my sexuality. After a mercifully short tongue kiss, she would usually pass out on my shoulder, leaving me feeling protective and proud.

Aside from drunk driving, there were other dangers for a gay teenage alcoholic. I had persuaded my mother to buy me a tanning lamp and, after school, while my parents were still at work, I would work on my tan while getting drunk. My

preferred drink at the time was a toxic brew called a Strip-N-
Go-Naked, comprised of equal parts of frozen lemonade,
vodka, and beer. One day, after several of these cocktails, I became concerned that my parents might come home soon so I
took the sunlamp into the bathroom, filled up the tub, and
stretched out for a good tan. When the timer on the lamp
went off, I was already quite pink but decided to go for another ten minutes. Reaching up, I hit the cord of the lamp
and watched it fall toward me in the bathtub. I very clearly
remember my life being saved that day. The lamp fell toward
me in slow motion and something lifted me up and out of
the water just before it hit the water. The bulbs exploded as
they hit the water and the lights in the house surged before
the circuit breakers snapped off in the basement. I stood motion-
less in the pitch black of the windowless bathroom that day
for a long time before I cleaned up the broken glass.

My sexual preference had been fairly clear, if not very
welcome, in my mind at an early age. When I was no more
than nine or ten, I stole a *Playgirl* from the local drug store,
completely entranced by the heavy black moustache of the
model on the cover. The sight of his black hair and white skin
was hypnotic. I simply had to have it. The stealing of the magazine was one thing; being caught was another. The feel of
the store-owner's hand on my shoulder is burned into my
memory. He did nothing more than give me a good scolding
and sent me on my way but his words ignited a terror in me
of being found out.

By the time I was in junior high school, with the full
force of puberty hitting me, I realized I could no longer ignore
my sexuality. Television became unbearable. It seemed designed
to torture me. With each glimpse of a man's arm or a hairy
leg, I was engulfed with both desire and shame. As time went
on, the pressure to act on my sexual needs became too pow-

erful to ignore. In high school, liquor allowed me to obliter-
ate consciousness and make a series of ill-considered passes at
boys. Sadly, none of these attempts were ever consummated
but, perhaps because I made sure my target was always as
drunk as I, they also never resulted in me being beaten. My
greatest love was a short stocky blond (the first and only
blond I've ever desired) who had an athletic little body, not
much of a brain, and a brother who had been driven out of
town when his homosexuality was revealed. I figured there
was a good chance that the object of my affections had also
received the gay gene so, one night after many beers and *Star
Trek* reruns, I made my move. I dimly recall a tentative touch,
a mumbled confession and his head turning away from me.
When I saw him the next day and handed him his home-
work, which I had completed for him as usual, neither of us
spoke of it.

I was eager to try anything that would relieve the boredom of life in Iowa and using drugs did not seem like an es-
calation from drinking but part of the same activity. Drugs
and alcohol certainly squelched some of the terror of being
gay in as homophobic a place as Iowa but, ultimately, I think
I used them to add some kind of sparkle to the dullness of
those gray cornfields. It was just so damn boring there. Although I can't recall my first drug, other than Dexitrim, it
was probably pot because it was readily available. Addicts are
nothing if not resourceful in their search for drugs. In Cherokee, Iowa, population barely scraping 6,000, I found every
drug except cocaine and heroin. Pot was a no-brainer and
easy to obtain. Not much of a smoker, I preferred pot and
hash mixed into a stir-and-bake chocolate cake. There were a
variety of pills that delivered a rush of speed: Robin's Eggs
and Black Beauties were favorites but a fistful of Dexitrim
would frankly do just as well in a pinch. With my bad girl

posse, I would gag down fists of dried mushrooms that some-times yielded mild hallucinations but, at other times, simply made us vomit for hours. And somehow the town sheriff's daughter had a large supply of poppers that we would snort while whirling around the floor at school dances.

Best of all was good old blotter acid. I recall Green Pyramids, which were powerful hits of LSD pressed into some sort of green crystalline substance that would melt on our tongues. Our tiny world became mysterious and fascinating on acid. An evening at the V.F.W. with my parents was suddenly an ad-venture. Getting lost on a walk around the block could oc-cupy an entire afternoon. Staci and I would sit in my basement, listening to David Bowie, and dancing while the walls melted.

There was plenty of unexamined rage in our drug adven-tures. Staci and I had a favorite game, exhilarating but rarely played because of its danger. She had a beat-up Pinto Cruising Wagon, which I thought was the height of chic at the time. It was the color of a cherry tomato and had little portholes on either side in back rather than traditional windows. There were so many dents in the car that new ones were hardly notice-able. At the time, car lots were open at night in Iowa so that prospective buyers could cruise around viewing the merchan-dise. Although brightly lit, they were completely unattended late at night. After a few thermoses of Strip-N-Go-Nakeds and a hit of blotter acid each, Staci and I would head to the car lots. We would cruise past the sparkling cars, pretending to consider them, even having little pretend conversations.

Staci would park a few feet away from the Lincoln and coo, "Oh, honey, I think that Lincoln Continental is just di-vine. And it'll be perfect when we have kids."

I would take another slug from the thermos and growl, "You got a bun in the oven, baby? I knew I shouldn't fuck you."

She would casually look around the lot for any sign of activity. She rubbed her belly suggestively, "I think I got twins cookin' in here."

"You whore. We'd better make sure that car's big enough. Get up closer."

Staci gunned the motor. "Want me to get closer?"

"Closer, bitch!"

"Real close?" Staci flashed her high beams.

"Get right up on that fucker!" I'd scream. "Let's go!"

Staci would stomp on the gas and shift into gear, the Pinto's tires screaming as we hurtled forward a few feet into the new car. Slam! We would sit there for a minute afterward, shocked and spent, almost like we'd just had sex. Then we would drive off without another word.

Because I've stayed in contact with so few of my high school friends, including Staci, I have no way of knowing how many of them moved on to addiction. For them, it may well have been a passing phase. For me, it was a powerful start to an experiment that would span nearly twenty years. The little black pills, the mysterious potions, the sparkling powders, and the glittering shards of acid were all means of escape. In those childhood years, I was sure that the bleak prospects for a gay boy in Iowa were the problem. Even if I didn't have a clear picture of what my adult life would have looked like had I stayed in Iowa, the daily taunts of "faggot" in school and the occasional bloody nose from some young thug who caught me looking at him gave me a good idea. I must have been far more effeminate as a young man than I thought because I never came out in Iowa . . . everyone just knew. But Iowa was only the first good excuse for getting loaded. Later, the rushing intensity of New York was the reason for my pain. Yet, when I reached Los Angeles, the same isolation and insanity was waiting for me.

I close the photo album and turn off the lamp in my office. Usually, I can hear the roar of traffic from La Cienega Boulevard but tonight there is only silence. Then, as often happens in Los Angeles at dusk, the mockingbirds begin to sing. Los Angeles is a strange amalgam: domesticated and wild; metropolitan and suburban; superficial and spiritual all mixed together beyond recognition. During the day, wild parrots, descendents of escaped pet birds, flock into the trees near my house, all flashes of violent green and hoarse cries. A huge white egret, miles from the nearest body of water appropriate to its size, occasionally appears in my backyard, a lawn ornament come to life, wading into the small pool to gobble down my goldfish. Possums, rats, raccoons, and skunks scratch at my roof in the night before jostling the garbage cans. I live in the flats of Los Angeles but, in the Hollywood Hills, the juxtaposition is even more dramatic as hawks swoop down to grab tabby cats, coyotes stalk poodles, and mountain lions watch hungrily as joggers traverse the canyon trails.

The rain has stopped when I leave the house for a walk but it is cold in the early evening gloom. I have fallen in love with my iPod and I insert its little cushioned speakers into my ears. The birdsongs disappear as I trail my finger around the face of the machine to raise the volume and the night becomes a movie, complete with my personally created soundtrack. The music is deafening inside my head but absolutely undetectable to the outside world.

It's dark here on the edges of West Hollywood, far away from the flickering lights of Santa Monica Boulevard. Thunderheads still mass along the hills but here, in the center of the basin, the stars are clearly visible in the night sky. There is a new moon and I have a vague memory that a new moon brings dramatic change. It's cold enough tonight that I can see my breath so I pull my leather jacket tight around me. With Madonna bleating out, "... it's like a little prayer," I walk into the dark.

Chapter 4

DINO

Judy's office is a mass of paperwork: small mountains leaning against the wall, others arranged into some obscure order on her desk. This visual reminder of the more mundane parts of her job doesn't seem to bother Judy. She just kicks back, her feet on top of the nearest pile, and stretches her long arms over her head.

She runs her finger down a resident list, "Liar, big liar, liar, getting better."

"What about Ding-Dong?"

Judy's face lights up. "He's doin' great."

"Should I . . . call him Ding-Dong?"

"What everybody calls him."

I stare out the window at a palm tree that looks as if it's trying to free itself from the earth. The rains have paused today and a gusty wind has cleared sections of deep blue California sky but a few blue-black thunderheads are still rolling along the hills.

"He makes me uncomfortable."

Judy doesn't follow-up on this but smacks her sensible shoe down just in time to pin an errant government report to the desk as it begins to slide to the floor. I know she'll wait me out so I might as well just be out with it. "You know . . . he reminds me of my lover . . . Dino. Died of AIDS."

On one level, Ding-Dong bears absolutely no resemblance to Dino, other than being a middle-aged man eaten away by disease. Ding-Dong has spent years on the street and wears clothes that tend to be shades of dirty beige whereas Dino was always wrapped in rich layers of deeply colored wool. It's Ding-Dong's cough and angry resignation that remind me of Dino. Just before Ding-Dong doubles over, hacking away, there's a moment when his milky white eyes flash with anger. He knows the cough well by now, an unwelcome friend, and also knows that it won't be leaving. Still there's a moment of challenge, a drawing up as if to say, "Are you back already?"

Long after he was too sick to comfortably go to such places, Dino would insist on going to wildly expensive and chic Manhattan restaurants for dinner. The urbane patrons would not allow themselves to appear shocked at the sight of Dino's bone-thin but well-dressed form staggering across the dining room. However, at some point in the meal, despite a heavy dose of Hycodan syrup, he would always begin to cough. Wet and rattling, it was what is called a productive cough. He would cover his mouth with an elegant white hankie, his eyes challenging the stares of diners at nearby tables, daring them to stare or move to another table.

Judy has the ability to wait through a silence without any apparent discomfort. If this were Group, she'd let the feeling gnaw at me until I spit it out but, as a friend, she gives me a little prod. "Does he make you afraid?"

"I don't know."

In nearly every room of the House, a laminated poster titled "How Do You Feel?" is prominently displayed. An illustrated version of the "Feelings List" that each resident carries around, the poster has thirty or forty little circles on it, each given a slightly different expression and labeled underneath with a different emotion. The "happy" face is instantly recognizable as are the narrowed eyes and down-turned mouth of "angry." The wide eyes of "afraid" are joined by an open mouth to signify "shocked."

I can feel that my face is red and I don't know why because the story of my ex-lover is no secret. I've told it many times in front of hundreds of people in Twelve-step meetings. But somehow, here, it seems shameful, as if it's something I've been hiding.

"Maybe I should start using a Feelings List," I laugh.

"Why not?" Judy asks flatly as she reaches forward to pluck one from a towering pile near her knee. She holds it out and I take it but I don't need to look at it because I know how I feel.

"Ashamed."

I exported myself from Iowa the day after high school graduation, hoping to get as far east as possible, preferably New York City. However, New York University was not suitably impressed with me and, in rejecting my application, probably saved my life. Instead, I landed in Pittsburgh with two goals—getting drunk and getting laid—both of which I achieved brilliantly.

I thought I wanted to be a theater director but soon found that the razzle-dazzle of Carnegie-Mellon's theater department was not for me. Not quite willing to give up on theater, I added in enough lit classes to also qualify as a morose English Literature major. Because most of my nights were spent drinking and my mornings were devoted to recovering from hangovers, I had little time to study. Fortunately, I'd always been good at tests so I still managed to get decent grades while learning next to nothing. I spent the next two years, until I was a junior, haunting the gay clubs of Pittsburgh, picking up several cases of gonorrhea, and looking for love.

Then I met Constantine Zachary Moraitis—Dino—standing in an ugly little gay bar down the hill from Carnegie-Mellon University in Pittsburgh. Actually, I didn't meet him that first night but saw him from across the room. By the time I'd gotten drunk enough to talk to him, he was gone. The second time I saw Dino, he was magically hanging out with a group of friends whom I'd gone to the bar to meet. Though I had no idea what my type was at that point, Dino was completely and utterly it. A Greek, there was something exotic about his beautiful, dark eyes framed by thick lashes and his furry arms. Yet he was dressed like a Brooks Brothers advertisement in an old buttoned-down shirt, madras shorts, and a battered gold Rolex, which I learned later was a fake. He wore the strangest shoes I'd ever seen. They were called Clarke's Wallabees and they looked like little brown boxes encasing his feet. He was fascinating. Most of all, though, I loved the way he smelled; he was doused, practically floating in a cloud, of Guerlain Vetiver.

I fell deeply in love for the first time and was fascinated by this man to such an extent that I really wanted to become him. Dino wasn't butch but he was eccentric in a masculine way. He had an odd, duck-footed walk and his upper lip would sweat with pleasure when he ate. I would later come to love his family. They had weathered a series of tragedies that lived up to their Greek heritage. Dino's mother was dying of cancer when I met him, and his brother, a brilliant young doctor, had been horribly murdered in an S/M sex scene a few years earlier. Dino's father was a miniature version of his son, accurately predicting Dino's future course of shrinkage, but relatively unbowed by the tragedy in his life. Most of all, I loved Dino's elder sister who was a voluptuous Greek woman with a voice like a bell. Wrapped in flowing dresses, with long black hair and tinkling gold jewelry, she was an earth mother version of Maria Callas. Dino had just graduated from Yale with a master's degree in classics and had returned home because of his mother's illness. He worked in his sister's restaurant, shopped, and hit the bars.

On the first night I spoke with Dino, one of us asked the other on a date the next evening. At the time, I was off from school for the summer and working as a waiter in a chic French restaurant on the still industrial South Side of Pittsburgh. In the afternoons, I would ride my bike from Shadyside down past the Carnegie Institute, the University of Pittsburgh and, finally, along the border of the city's poor black neighborhood—the Hill District. Although Pittsburgh was no longer a steel town, a few of the mills were still in operation in the early '80s and their outlines formed a surreal backdrop along the Monongahela River. As night fell, the mills would glow, belching smoke and fire from deep within their bellies.

For our first date, Dino was to pick me up at a bar on the South Side after I got off work. I waited at the bar for fifteen minutes and, when he didn't show, I figured he was a flake. This was, of course, before cell phones and patience has never been one of my virtues. I left on my bike, pedaling angrily back over the bridge toward town. Dino pulled alongside me halfway over the bridge, driving an old yellow station wagon and full of apologies. I think he was probably impressed that I hadn't waited longer for him and I was definitely impressed when he insisted on loading my bike into the back of his wagon, immediately christened the Banana Boat, and drove me home. Though he also carried my bike up the stairs to my apartment that night, I would later find that Dino was not in the habit of lifting anything. But that night he was the perfect gentleman and it all began.

We spent that summer and my senior year of college eating and drinking. Dino wasn't much for drugs and neither was I at the time, although I'd developed a taste for cocaine when I could afford it. At the time, coke was the kind of drug that prompted all-night, intense talks with close friends rather than the degrading fuck fests it would later inspire. We preferred Dewars and sodas in seedy lounges with black leather banquettes and an elderly chanteuse draped over the piano, wheezing out standards. We slept together in the single bed in my dorm room most nights, tightly wrapped around one another.

At Thanksgiving Dino took me to New York for the first time and we stayed at the St. Regis. I didn't understand at the time that Dino wasn't really rich because I had no sense that there were levels of wealth. There were people like Dino who enjoyed luxury, and with his small inheritance along with money from his father, an eye surgeon, he plunged into the velvety excess of New York when he could. For me, New York was a world of impossible glamour and Dino unlocked it effortlessly. On that weekend in New York, we ate the first of many meals at the old La Côte Basque, strolled through Central Park, and bought Vetiver at Bergdorf Goodman.

I didn't encounter the sexual, draining side of New York on that first trip because I was wrapped in the safety of being deeply in love. When we wandered through the streets of the Village, the city was a postcard. Even had I known they existed, I would have had no interest in the crumbling industrial buildings that held the Mineshaft and the Hellfire a few blocks away. Instead, I walked down the windy streets holding Dino's hand, content with what I had. And, for his part, Dino was entirely focused on me and touched at being able to introduce me to this new world. Where I would have trembled before the formidable sales clerks, Dino flung open the door to A La Vielle Russie to show me a Fabergé egg, pulled me into J. Press on Madison to try on a sports coat, and at Bergdorf's flirted with the sales girl who told me I had beautiful skin. It seemed perfect but, had I wanted to, I could have already seen the beginnings of trouble.

For one thing, there was an old boyfriend from Yale that still hovered on the horizon. Although it would be years before I actually met Bob Works, he seemed like a formidable competitor. He went by the nickname of "Works" and was an architect in Boston, bi-sexual, with an enormous member that was apparently documented in a series of photographs displayed in his apartment. Dino never seemed to think of him as an actual boyfriend but Works remained tantalizingly on the horizon as an escape route from our relationship. A few times a year, Dino would disappear to New York or Boston to meet Works and I would hunker down in despair. Only when Works finally announced that he was engaged to be married, did it seem that the final barrier to our life together had been removed.

Dino was not the only one who kept some action on the side. Like many men in their early twenties, I simply felt incapable of monogamy but was also too afraid that, if I confessed to Dino that I wanted another arrangement, I would lose him. In fact, because he was fucking around, Dino would probably have welcomed a looser arrangement. I also believed that the kind of rough, aggressive sex I was becoming interested in could only be had anonymously or during quick affairs. For that kind of sex I sought out older, powerful guys who were walking stereotypes of masculinity. One such man was a rugged professor with a floppy moustache and a fisherman's cap who I pursued through my senior year at Carnegie. At the time, there were occasional parties on campus where students and professors would get dead drunk together in one of the old mansions near campus that housed visiting faculty. At one such party, I finally bedded my fantasy man but remembered little other than the raging hangover that greeted me when I woke up in his bed the next morning. I'd lost my contact lenses, vomited in his bathroom, and was, most likely, a cautionary tale for him regarding future teacher/student dalliances.

Whether it was a result of one of my local flings or one of Dino's trips to New York, we both developed hepatitis B. Our response was the first of our lies by omission. We simply never discussed how we had become infected. For a few weeks, Dino retired to a hospital, very ill, while I, equipped with a Herculean immune system, simply felt tired. Once we had both recovered, we stopped drinking for a while and never spoke of it again.

As my senior year drew to a close, I decided that I would move to New York. The city the most likely place to get a job in the theater, which was ostensibly my career plan, but it also had other attractions. It wasn't just that I wanted to move to a gay city—San Francisco and Los Angeles never occurred to me—New York also represented all that was dark and rough as well as chic and glamorous. I simply assumed that Dino would be eager to come with me. Rather, he began a torrid affair with an egg-headed local sculptor who, financed by his family's money, had been living in Rome. After much screaming and guilt-inducing tears—he could never bear to see me cry—Dino drove me to my new apartment in the Banana Boat but made it clear that he was going to Rome with the sculptor and had no interest in living in New York.

Once Dino had departed for Rome with the sculptor, I was left in a small apartment with three roommates and a job as New York's worst waiter. I had a fantasy of New York that had little to do with the grinding reality of living there without immense amounts of money. I thought that I was equipped to play in the city's sexual wonderland, fueled by drugs, but found them to be more complicated than I had expected. In 1984, AIDS was certainly known, even in Pittsburgh, but it was not central in my thoughts about sex and I never used a condom with Dino. When tricking, I practiced a loose version of safe sex but, with Dino, I convinced myself that something about being in love with him protected me and, besides, the idea of either one of us already being infected was too terrifying to even consider. It was as if I vanquished that thought through the act of having unsafe sex with him.

The world of gay New York that I arrived into had already been crippled and twisted by the mounting death toll. However, I rushed in thinking that it was still whole and not realizing that I was walking through a funeral. But there was always an edgy feeling that held me back from losing myself entirely. Perhaps I would have gone further had I really felt single; I had a brief affair and lots of anonymous sex but I was waiting for Dino. With all that happened between us, I was always sure that he was "the one." Within six months, Dino's mother died and his infatuation with the sculptor in Rome lessened. By the following fall, we were living together in a loft on Twenty-second Street near the Flatiron Building. I don't know if he moved to New York because he loved me or if he simply didn't know what else to do.

Our early days in New York together were slow and dreamy. Dino, unsure of his career aspirations, still grieving from his mother's death, and never the most ambitious person anyway, spent his days trailing through stores and waiting for me to get home from my waiter job. I was probably one of the few lunch-shift waiters in New York who, in the evenings, ate regularly at the Four Seasons. With its stark modernism and undulating curtains of metal beads, the restaurant, my favorite, erased any memory of being a white trash boy from Iowa. It was as strange and wonderful to me as *Alice in Wonderland* was as a child; this was a place where silver trays of cotton candy were presented to diners celebrating a birthday. As I became more involved in the New York art world, I began to realize the value of the huge Rosenquist canvas and the Picasso tapestry that decorated the walls. I hadn't yet become jaded enough to worry that lunch was the time to be seen at the Four Seasons, while dinner was about tourists and high-priced hookers. I never noticed any famous faces but Dino, never one for traditional celebrities, once flushed with excitement and whispered to me, "Don't look now but it's MacArthur's widow."

We walked constantly in New York, exploring every inch of Manhattan. Autumns were particularly beautiful and Dino would sometimes take me to a strange hulking resort in New Paltz called the Mohonk Mountain House to look at the turning leaves. In the ramshackle Victorian hotel, we would sit in front of a fireplace and look at fall storms rolling toward us from across the valley.

Courtesy of his father's credit cards, Dino showed me the world and he always traveled in style. Although he flew coach, he loved the luxury of great hotels and taught me that they can transform a normal trip into a fantasy. Over the next nine years we stayed at Claridge's in London, the George V in Paris, the Hotel du Cap in the south of France, the Grande Bretagne in Athens, the Hassler in Rome, the Pera Palas in Istanbul and the Gritti Palace in Venice. Our first trip together was to Egypt and we checked into the Mena House in the shadow of the Giza pyramids before traveling down to the legendary Cataract Hotel in Aswan. From our room in Aswan, we could see

Elephantine Island and the white sails of feluccas gliding along the Nile.

At some point in each of these beautiful hotels, I would look out at an incredible vista and know that something was wrong. Why was I so unhappy sitting in the center of everything I had ever hoped for? Neither of us was drinking on those first trips; although we rarely visited a doctor, we were both still scared by the harm we'd likely done to our livers. Vacations tend to make me crazy because, without my daily routine, I'm left with myself. I have little interest in trailing through churches and ruins to look at the past, preferring instead to simply walk through the city. For someone who would later work in the art world, I also have a short attention span for museums. In short, without alcohol and drugs, I was a brooding nightmare during our trips.

We were sitting in the bar of the Hotel Cecil in Alexandria when we decided to drink again. Suddenly, a trip that had seemed like a disaster became carefree under the influence of Negronis and green Chartreuse. Dino had introduced me to Chartreuse in Pittsburgh and I had, at first, been revolted by its medicinal flavor but was intrigued by the burning sensation it created in my throat and the intense buzz it gave me. The liquor is a distant cousin to absinthe, which also made it irresistibly glamorous to me.

So, after Alexandria, we would drink on our trips and things would improve until I drank too much. Then, late at night, when Dino was either asleep or pretending to be asleep, I would go out to roam the city. I betrayed Dino in the alleyways of southern France, in the park on the Capitoline Hill in Rome, in the hammams of Istanbul, and the late movie theaters of Alexandria. When I returned from these walks, there was never a scene or even a comment, but I could tell that

Dino was not really asleep in the bed. I would slide into bed beside him, with the filth of other men still on me, and hold him, knowing full well that I had betrayed him but unable or unwilling to ask him for help.

My exploits were not limited to exotic foreign lands. They played out on an almost daily basis in the sex clubs, movie theaters, porn shops and streets of New York. As our life together came to an end, I betrayed Dino even in our own bed when he was visiting his family. And he did the same to me. One afternoon when I was home alone and making a half-hearted effort at cleaning the apartment, I glimpsed a slip of paper sticking out of a book on the shelf. Most of our books were from Dino's days at Yale and I had no reason to open the volumes of Aeschylus, Euripides, and Homer, all in ancient Greek. But Dino apparently had used the books almost daily during his time in New York. Stuck in the pages of *The Iliad*, *The Odyssey*, and *Lysistrata* were hundreds of slips of paper, each with a different man's name and telephone number scribbled on it. As I opened book after book, Dino's sexual history rained down around my feet. When I fucked other guys, I justified it as being just about sex and having nothing to do with my love for Dino. On one level, I was even proud of my promiscuity, believing that it set me aside from the mundane constraints of the straight world. But on that winter afternoon in New York I knew all my sexual bravado was bullshit. I sat down on the floor, surrounded by the fragile remnants of Dino's passionate sexual encounters with other men, and cried. I realized that each of those numbers in fact represented falling a little bit in love with another man. In total, we'd both loved other people so much that we didn't have enough love left for one another. After crying for a while, I carefully put the slips of paper back in the books, put the books on the shelf, and never confronted Dino anymore than he confronted me.

The shame I feel in the present has little to do with the drug-fueled sexual compulsion of my past. We were even on that count. It rises from the knowledge that as I dove into the haze of drugs I abandoned Dino emotionally in the last days of his life and, though I may have been there physically, he probably felt alone. No, I know better than that. He told me that he did. One late Sunday afternoon when I was still asleep, hungover after a late night that had stretched on until morning, he sat on the bed next to me and put his hand on my head. He was already very sick, his days consumed by doctors and medication, when he said to me sadly, "I always thought the point of having a lover is that I wouldn't feel alone." Not a day goes by that his words don't ring in my mind.

Our life changed one day in the late '80s when Dino and I were staying at a friend's house in the Fire Island Pines. Our sex had already become infrequent and I was trying hard to ignore his rapid weight loss, which began as a diet but had taken on an unstoppable momentum. I was already fairly drunk that afternoon when we went to our room to take a nap. I wanted to have sex, wanted to connect with him somehow, erase all the lies and start over. He turned away from me and pulled down his pants. I took it as an invitation but he began to cry and stuttered, "I have this . . . this thing on my ass. I don't think we should have sex anymore until I find out what it is."

I remember that thing so well. It was clearly not a mole. I knew from the moment I looked at it that the smooth brownish black stain on his buttock was a lesion and that all the force of what I'd stupidly believed we'd avoided was about to slam into us. Within two weeks, there was a diagnosis and the endless round of hospitals and doctors that would stretch on for the next two years had begun. There was absolutely no reason to believe that I would be negative. In fact, my belief that I was sick was reinforced by my initial test results being lost. After nearly a month of waiting for the results of the first test and then finally having another done, a belief that I was myself ill had become cemented in my mind and would take many years to dislodge despite numerous HIV tests. I would lie in bed at night, in sheets soaked by Dino's night sweats, trying to heal myself and force the illness, which was never even there, out of me. The daily terror of my belief that I was sick was deadened only a bit by an avalanche of white powder, pills, and cocktails.

There were moments during the process of Dino's dying when I was proud of myself. Although Dino was uninterested in activism and already resigned to his death, I found release, even inspiration, in the early years of ACT UP. I was arrested several times during large protests and one day after coming home from jail, Dino folded me in his arms and told me that I was his hero. Those words stay in my mind along with the more shameful ones.

But mostly I was in a haze of drugs during Dino's illness that allowed me to feel nothing but craving. I tried my best to hide my addiction from Dino but it must have been apparent to him as my using increased. His father had given me Fiorinal for my migraines and the powerful muscle relaxant became a daily aid. I also swirled Dino's tincture of opium into my evening drinks. Up to that point, cocaine had been only an occasional treat because of its expense. However, I ran into an old friend one day who looked thin and exhausted. I asked him what he'd been doing and he replied, deadpan, "A lot of blow." He assured me that his dealer had the cheapest coke in town and would deliver. I've since come to believe that my experiences with crystal began in those endless white packets delivered to my apartment because what little coke was in them was often supplemented by something infinitely more powerful. This was not the cheap coke I'd sometimes had before that had been cut with laxative and ground-up speed. This coke had a nasty yellowish cast to it sometimes and I stayed high for days.

Whether it was coke or crystal, I loved the feeling of a little brown vial of white powder in my pocket. Every few moments, I would put my hand in my pocket to reassure myself that the magic talisman was still there. I soon became a connoisseur of public restrooms in New York, favoring those that were large with multiple stalls; there was too much pressure to get quickly in and out of a "one-seater" bathroom with someone always waiting on the other side of the door. In a large, noisy restroom, no one kept track of the many minutes I spent in the stall. There I could leisurely examine the level in my vial and calculate exactly how much high time the amount of powder represented. Then, as a culmination of the ritual, I would snort several large lines laid out carefully on a credit card or the toilet paper holder.

Sometimes, of course, I didn't have the luxury of buying drugs and taking them home to chop up. I was once waiting for a delivery from my dealer when Dino announced that he wanted to go for tea at the Pierre. I told him that I would go downstairs and get a taxi to wait for us. A few moments later, my dealer arrived, handed me the drugs and disappeared just before Dino tottered out of the door wrapped in a huge Brooks Brothers overcoat. By the time we arrived at the Pierre, I had fondled the tiny package in my pocket a thousand times. Although he was very, very ill, Dino still loved the old ladies and the murals in the oval room where the Pierre served high tea. With his sunken cheeks and huge glasses perched on his bony nose, he staggered into the room oblivious of the stares from the ladies in their discreet Chanel suits. For me, their stares were like scalding water and I escaped to the bathroom as soon as we had ordered.

As was usual in elegant New York hotels, there was an elderly black man who was the attendant in the bathroom. In my tweed jacket and Hermes tie, he saw me not as a drug addict but someone who belonged in such a place. He simply smiled and nodded his head. I headed to a stall but knew that the room was far too quiet to chop up the drugs with a credit card and snort them. I took down my soft, elegant corduroy pants and sat on the toilet. As time passed, I stared at the glassine envelope and became progressively more paranoid that the bathroom attendant was becoming suspicious of my behavior. In that quiet, quiet bathroom, I silently unfolded the paper and stared at the whitish rocks. When I heard the attendant clear his throat, I panicked. Without further hesitation, I plucked the largest rock from the sachet, reached between my legs and stuffed it up my ass.

When I returned to the table a few minutes later, Dino was looking pensively at a cucumber sandwich. As I crossed the room toward him, it felt as if a hot knife was slowly tracing itself up and down my spine.

Dino died on the thirtieth of October in 1993 at the age of thirty-two. I had been snorting steadily, drinking, and taking Valium. In the preceding months, he had transferred the remainder of his money to me because, were I to ever probate the will he had written naming me as sole beneficiary, I would have had to pay his, by then, extensive credit card debts. I had already begun to mail-order clothes with his credit cards in the months before his death, anticipating that the companies would be unable to collect on the debt. The greed I felt for the money and clothes helped me not to think for a few hours and allowed me to focus on something tangible I might still get out of the situation.

The morning of his death I'd had to carry Dino to the toilet for the first time during his illness. For several days, he had been lying in bed with his eyes open but not seeing. I knew he was dying. His eyes were still beautiful that morning. I was admiring them when I saw one of his still thick eyelashes floating in his eye. When I tried to get it out, he thought that I had somehow decided to remove his eyelashes and moaned, "Don't take my eyelashes too."

I don't remember much of the day after that. He lay there dying and I could no longer go in to look. I sat in the living room drunk and high. A friend who'd come over finally came in to say, "I think he's dead." I cried and I kissed Dino and I closed his eyes but I was glad it was over.

The morning after my first true love died I stole his credit cards, got drunk, snorted some blow, called a car service, and went shopping. It was the best I could do at that moment. With the passing comfort of a new suit, a computer or two, and a few more lines, I mourned Dino as I had watched him die. I wasn't really there.

By the time I returned home that night, I was close to passing out. My hired car, filled with stolen goods, pulled up in front of my building. When the driver opened the door, I saw a tall bright-red devil strolling down the street. He leered at me and stuck out his tongue. For a moment, I thought I had gone insane or had been transported to hell, where I belonged. Then I realized that it was simply Halloween in Greenwich Village. Hell was yet to come.

Judy's not one for handholding. In response to the tears streaming down my face, she hands me not a tissue but a bag of Depends adult diapers. I note that they are the "new snug-fitting briefs." She winks at me and nods.

"Judy, I'm fucked up. Not incontinent."

"Ding-Dong's both fucked up and incontinent. Maybe you should help him out. He's an actual person, you know."

"Of course, I know that."

Judy's beaming now and that usually means she's come up with a solution. As I feel my stomach churning, I know she's willing to just sit there and wait me out.

"What do I say to him?" I regret it immediately.

"Something like . . . I've got your diapers, Ding-Dong. Need some help?"

I retreat from her office with the Depends banging against my leg like a bale of hay. They're incredibly light for their size but Judy likes to buy in bulk and there must be a hundred in the package.

In the front hall, the residents are milling around, finished with their chores but reluctant to dive into morning Group. They don't trust me yet so most are content to nod and keep their distance. I ask Tommy, a little bald guy who I used to know from A.A. meetings, "You see Ding-Dong?"

He regards me for a moment with my bale of diapers and nods, "Upstairs gettin' dressed."

I've never been upstairs and feel like I'm trespassing as I plod up the central staircase. Four large bedrooms, converted into dormitories, open off the hallway. I decide the first must be for the girls because it is painted Pepto-Bismol pink. Down the hall is another bedroom but the door is closed. From inside, I hear a wracking cough and, then, soft muttering, "Fuck. God damn it."

I knock on the door. "Ding-Dong? You in there?"

The rustling stops. Silence. I open the door slowly and see Ding-Dong sitting on the side of a bunk bed, completely naked except for a pair of underwear twisted around one ankle that he yanks at without much hope. I haven't seen a body in this condition since Dino. His arms are so impossibly thin that it looks as if the bones of his elbows and shoulders will tear through the papery, sallow skin. Only a few desultory wisps of hair remain around his shrunken cock.

Ding-Dong hasn't had a chance to pull back his hair and it hangs in his face, making him look mostly like a shorn, emaciated sheep dog. He abandons the underwear and pushes the hair back from his face. His eyes are milky white, covered in filmy cataracts. He peers into the room, "Who's that?"

"Patrick."

"Hmm." Ding-Dong just waits to see what will happen. This is what his years on the street have taught him—don't struggle, just see what happens.

"Um . . . Judy told me to bring these up to you. See if you need any help." I hold up the Depends, wiggling them a little like a play toy in front of a kitten.

Ding-Dong tilts his head. "I can't see, Patrick."

"Oh, right. They're Depends."

Ding-Dong struggles to his feet and prances a bit, singing the jingle from the Depends commercial. Then he just stands, arms slack, next to the bed, staring silently.

"Let me unwrap 'em for you." I tear at the Depends and find that they are vacuum-packed. The bundle begins to expand as it fills with air. "Fuck, Ding-Dong, there must be about a thousand of 'em in here."

"Good, 'cause I'm full of shit."

"That you are, honey." I extract a pair of diapers finally. It looks like a pair of puffy briefs.

Ding-Dong looks blankly into the middle distance but his voice is full of despair. "They're big. They make me look like . . ."

"Like you're wearing diapers, right?"

Ding-Dong nods. I put my hand on his bony, ice-cold shoulder and guide him back down onto the bed.

"Well," I say as I lean down and pull the tattered underwear off his ankle, "I know a thing or two about diapers and these happen to be the Rolls Royce of adult bladder control."

"Hmm." This seems to be Ding-Dong's indicator that he's willing to listen but unconvinced.

"Because Ms. Judy has bought you the new snug-fit briefs, they're gonna feel like slipping into a pair of Calvin Kleins."

I begin to wiggle the diapers up Ding-Dong's body and I'm surprised that he doesn't smell. Somehow he still manages to bathe himself and little whiffs of cheap soap float off his body as I pull the Depends up past his cock.

Toward the end of his life, Dino's skeletal body, stripped of its easy muscularity, revolted me. Somehow I lost sight of him. I was grateful that Dino, being extremely fastidious, rarely allowed me to help him. To the end, he insisted on showering and bathing himself while I waited anxiously in the bathroom in the event he crashed to the floor. Touching the sharp angles and strange bulges of Ding-Dong's body, I realize how much I missed by not allowing myself this intimacy with Dino.

Ding-Dong puts his hand on my shoulder, "How do they look, Patrick?"

I step back from Ding-Dong. "Let me take a look."

Ding-Dong stands with a hand on his hip, coyly posing. He grins. Half his teeth are cracked off or black. His hair has fallen back down into his face like a wig that's been pulled on backward.

I step forward, pull out the elastic waistband of his new panties and give them a little snap. "Honey, you look like a million bucks."

Chapter 5

GOOD TIMES

I've acquired my first circuit boy sponsee, Evan, and he wants nothing more than to dance. Each day he calls to tell me of another hot party that he could and should be attending that night. I usually settle in on the patio to clip my fingernails when he calls because I know it will be a long trajectory, starting with his anger that this central pleasure in his life, dancing, has been denied him. We will then move on to the realization, new again in his tweaker brain, that he will likely use if he is surrounded by hundreds of sweating men snorting drugs. And the cycle will repeat the following week when he sees a poster with a hot shirtless boy advertising the latest party: the Black Party, the White Party, the Black & Blue, the FireBall, Prizm, Sweat, or Forbidden. Evan subscribes to *Circuit Noize* and spends hours on-line studying the photos of hairless, muscle "boyz" grinding their teeth as they smile for the camera or throwing their arms to the sky as they dance under an endless succession of disco balls.

My job is to remind Evan that a few months ago he was found wandering, psychotic, and muttering to himself on the streets of Santa Monica. Only in his early thirties, Evan had burned through a high-paying job as a chemist for a large drug manufacturer while making crystal for himself. His short career as a cooker started with making just enough crystal to keep him and a coterie of young muscle gods high for a few days of dancing in expensive beach houses on Fire Island, the grounds of Miami's Viscaya, the dark theaters of New York, or the desert sands of Palm Springs. It seemed to Evan, traveling each weekend to another exotic destination to meet the same group of fantasy men, that life was perfect. He was smart in the beginning and never traveled with drugs. Rather he would FedEx them to the hotel where he was staying and, upon arrival, would distribute the party favors to his group. Some would pay and others, in his inner circle, would be given their favors for free. Evan grew very popular.

It is said that, for addicts, drugs are cunning, baffling, and powerful. Crystal is all that and cheap as well. Crystal first finds a way to fix all of the problems that we have and then, when it has made itself indispensable, reveals its true self. For Evan, the drug that took him out of the closet and placed him, relieved of shame, on a dance floor with the most beautiful men in the world, would later make him so paranoid that even if he made it to the city where the party was taking place, he was unable to leave his room. Instead, he would be trapped in the gleaming white, high-design room of some hotel with the blinds drawn, absolutely sure that a SWAT team had been deployed to the roofs of surrounding buildings, ready to pick him off like a bird in hunting season. Many weekends Evan would retreat to the darkness of hotel bathrooms, clothes closets, or even crawl under the bed if there was sufficient space to squeeze his big body into. He would spend hours searching for somewhere that was closed and protected from the whirling menace he felt outside.

Evan hadn't lost his job. Rather he quit, knowing that walking through the corporate labs, where real surveillance cameras followed his moves and a security badge flapped heavily on his chest, was untenable given the paranoia that accompanied his daily habit. Without a job, the days stretched endless before Evan and even two or three hours in the gym were insufficient to distract him from tweaking. Still, he was able to survive for a time by cooking crystal and selling it to his buddies who were still able to travel the circuit. Soon the gym dropped away as well and Evan's magnificent body began to wither, his golden skin took on a gray cast, and several teeth broke in half from the pressure of his jaw constantly grinding them together like mortar and pestle. As his drug psychosis increased, Evan became convinced that tiny microphones had been embedded in the walls of his apartment and he began to methodically pick the plaster off the walls using nothing more than his fingernails. Neighbors, convinced that the scratching was an indicator of rats in the walls, eventually insisted that the building's owner investigate the sounds. Unable to reach Evan by phone or persuade him to come to the door, the landlord had opened the door with his passkey to find Evan cowering in a corner of the living room, sheets taped over the windows, and the walls a destroyed, bloody mess. Evan's fingers had looked like scabby claws for months afterward.

But all that seems like nothing more than a bad dream to Evan when he gazes at the irresistible images of young gods, their bodies oiled and illuminated by golden light. And I understand how easy it must be for him to forget because his body, so young and strong, has magically healed itself. He looks now as if he has spent his life on a farm tending the soil, retiring early each evening and letting simple, fulfilling foods nourish his strong body. Without knowing that HIV coursed

through his body and that hepatitis C had permanently damaged his liver, one would think he was an aspiring movie star
or a model.

So Evan has called about a party called, appropriately
enough, Resurrection, which promises the cream of the circuit DJs and the world's most beautiful boyz. I am about to
begin clipping my big toenail and launch into my usual argu-
ments when he throws me a curve.

"Umm . . . Can I ask you a question?"

"What Evan?"

"Well, wasn't there that one . . . like . . . perfect night?"

"What do you mean?"

"Fucked up in a club and dancing. Music was just right
and it was like . . . perfect?"

"I don't know. You tell me."

"No, I mean for you. Like in New York . . . in the old
days."

"I'm not some ancient old hag, you know."

"I didn't mean . . ."

"I know, I know."

"So . . . was there?"

I sit still for a moment and consider lying. Then I put
down the nail clipper and sigh, "Yeah, I had that night."

In the six months I spent alone in New York while Dino
was in Rome, I went to clubs nearly every night. The club I
most wanted to enter was the most intimidating and it took
me several weeks after moving to the city before I could summon up the courage and cash to show up on Second Avenue
and Sixth Street on a Saturday night. On that corner, in an old
theater, sat what had, by 1984, become the center of the gay
universe. The Saint.

The Saint had opened to a rush of excitement in 1980 in the old Fillmore East, which had provided years of druggy nightlife to the fans of Janis Joplin and Jimmy Hendrix. By the mid '80s, when I arrived in New York, gay nightlife was imploding and the early AIDS deaths were already sapping the energy of night people. Although the Saint was well past its prime when I walked toward it that night, it still had attitude to spare. An intimidating leather daddy sprawled on a stool in front of a tiny door at the side of the building. He barely glanced up as he barked out, "Members only."

I had been intrepid in my research, phoning ahead to find out that the club had a policy of admitting, at their discretion, those with out-of-state drivers' licenses. Whether this had always been the policy or was a response to the thinning crowds inside, this was to be my salvation. I clutched my Iowa driver's license in my hand, praying that it would open the doors.

"But . . . I'm from out-of-town and they said . . ."

Leather daddy gave me a quick look over. What I lacked in style, I probably made up for in youth. It was ridiculously early, probably no later than 11:30, and there was no one else seeking admission. His big hairy hand flopped out, "Let me see."

I handed him the license and he gave it a glance. His brown eyes met mine for the first time. This man, fur sprouting from beneath a black tank top, seemed like a creature from another planet to me. His eyes narrowed.

"That shirt's not gonna work. Take it off."

Somehow I'd come up with a white button-down shirt and jeans as the fashion choice for the Saint. I was still wildly insecure about my body, carrying around the memory of my childhood fat like a phantom carcass, even though I was thin. I was hesitant to take off my shirt at the beach, let alone on a street in New York.

"Take it off?"

He held my gaze. There was no kindness in his eyes. He just waited.

I slowly unbuttoned my starched little shirt and began to shrug out of it. There was something humiliating about standing there, the hot air of the street wrapping around my exposed flesh.

The leather man said nothing. He just cocked his head toward the door.

Everything was of a piece at the Saint. The aesthetic of the place extended from the sloping entrance lobby to the starry reaches far above. That night, I found myself in a nearly empty hallway that had once been the theater's lobby. I paid what seemed like, on my limited funds, an extraordinary admission fee of twenty-five dollars, sullenly accepted by yet another leather man who stamped my hand and waved me in. A short man in a T-shirt manned the drycleaner style coat racks, which gleamed with silver hangers awaiting the night's sweaty clothes. After I surrendered another five dollars, he grabbed my shirt away and thrust a black plastic claim check into my hand.

I had an advantage that first night at the Saint because, for the first and last time, I entered the club sober. Not that I hadn't wanted to be high for the experience but I simply didn't have any more money, not even for a hit of blotter acid. Rather than the rushes of images and lost hours I would later associate with the club, my temporarily clear vision took in every detail of the club's carefully designed experience that night.

Pushing through yet another set of doors, I was in the downstairs lounge with a bar and modular units covered with industrial gray carpet upon which rested a few hirsute beauties, snorting assorted powders out of brown vials or throwing back pills. The room was an expanse of gray punctuated by towering floral displays on the bars. Television monitors, suspended in cages from the ceilings, played trippy visuals. Black iron staircases led upward but, for the moment, it was enough for me to stop and take in the atmosphere in that room. My discomfort at being shirtless was only intensified by the dark thickness of the bodies now wandering into the club. I arranged myself alongside the bar, leaning in such a way that I found cover for my love handles, crossed my arms to give my biceps some bulk and stretched my stomach muscles into a smooth curve. I needn't have worried so much as absolutely no one paid any attention to me. In fact, they paid very little attention to one another. They were intent on their preparations and themselves.

The men in attendance that night were my fantasies made flesh. They were everything that I had so long associated with New York. These were the clones of Fire Island or at least those who had not yet succumbed to the disease that was so relentlessly focused on their tiny population. That night they swaggered through the big steel doors into the lounge, their bodies slick with dark fur and hard faces set with dark eyes made more mysterious by the shadows of beards, moustaches, and rough stubble. Others glided in, already very high, and sailed straight through the room to carefully ascend the stairways, hanging on tight to the railings.

Something held me back from following the increasing stream that headed upstairs. Partly it was fear, in that I honestly did not know what waited for me above. I knew it was a dance floor but there was a gravity to these men that made them seem as if they were heading to worship in a church rather than to dance. They moved slowly and intently, as if in a processional that had clear stops and rituals prescribed for its successful completion.

I don't remember the music that night but I remember its constant, insistent beat that held all the images together. The music's intensity made conversation mostly impossible, which seemed better, as conversation in such a place would have been senseless. So I simply stood there as the club filled. Finally, a man, rail-thin and dressed head to toe in black leather, stalked to the center of the room. His head swiveled, as if expecting applause, and a few guys did actually nod in his direction. The leatherman climbed on top of a small mountain of gray cubes, reached inside his chaps, and drew out a bottle of poppers. I thought I could smell them from across the room as he drew one, two, three deep breaths off the bottle. From the belt of his chaps, he reached slowly for what appeared to be two long, silver batons. With a snap, they opened into gleaming silver fans. Now a few more heads turned to him and he angled his face up like an old actress catching the light. The music seemed to swell at that moment and the fans flew around him like huge, exotic moths as his body twisted and gyrated to the beat. His eyes were closed now and I thought, in that moment, that I must have gotten high from the scent of his poppers because my heart began to pound and the world seemed to fall away.

Enveloped by the smell of sweating men, I began to forget about my shirtless insecurities and finally made my way to a circular staircase. With each step up, the beat of the music grew more emphatic until, reaching the top, it was really not music anymore but a pounding inside of me. I emerged into a broad curved hallway, wide as an alley, and painted black. Towering above, though not fully revealed at that point, was an enormous dome, wrapped in a smooth parchment. The club, which had seemed nearly empty a few minutes before, had reached critical mass and the men shoved up against one another, both impatient and turned on. Surrounded by men

who, like me, were intent only on what they were approaching, I was sucked into the mouth of the dome's entrance.

When I entered the Saint's dome that first night it took
some time to understand what I saw. Even without drugs, I
felt as if I were flying into a starlit sky heavy with thunder. It
seemed that the building's roof had been removed to reveal
the night sky. The dome, without illumination, had disappeared
into limitless space and stars twinkled high, high above. On a
platform encircling the space, fan dancers swooped and crack-
led like fleshy insects with reflective wings. And, strangest and
most wonderful of all, was a huge protuberance, the star machine, which rose from the center of the dance floor, ominously swinging out its light speckled arms. This was the most
beautiful place I had ever been and, in some way that I didn't
yet understand, it was completely gay.

Eschewing the light shows seen in traditional discos, the
Saint installed a professional star machine that projected galax-
ies above while sweating, shirtless gods worshipped below. I
joined the dance that night without hesitation because, for all
the chilliness of the Saint's men, the floor was open to everyone. I moved for hours that night, from one group of men to
another, never connecting but never being excluded.

Time disappeared at the Saint but it seemed that hours
had passed without the dome changing. Yet, because it was so
beautiful, it was not monotonous. Later, much later, I realized
that lights had begun to illuminate the inside of the dome,
transforming it from a night sky to a perfect, seamless enclosure. It was still dark inside but somehow the sky had become
white. A hole opened in the eggshell above me and a cheer
rose up from the men as they continued to move in their low,
swinging dance. The stars dimmed, twinkled and faded. The
huge arms of the machine swung inward as if it were bowing
to approaching royalty. Out of the hole an enormous, mir-

rored ball descended into the dome, glittering darkly as it re-
volved slowly on high. The sky had been fixed all evening.
There had been no motion above, only the intricate patterns
of the men on the dance floor. Then a spotlight hit the rotating ball and thousands of beams of light reflected back into
space, moving slowly and steadily. The world began to spin
and I felt myself stumble a bit, disoriented by the movement
around me.

I left the dance floor for only a few moments that night.
Without any chemical rush, not even the poppers that men
sometimes offered to me, I danced for hours, transfixed by
the place. I didn't wear a watch in those years so I had no idea
how many hours, even days might have passed. At one point,
I left to drink water and take a piss and saw another stairway
leading up beyond the dome. Following the soaked, glistening bodies that glided up the steps, I found myself in the Saint's
balcony, looking out over the curve of the dome. Lit from within, the dome was a transparent scrim stretched over a skeleton
of industrial steel and filled with moving bodies far below. The
enormity of the place filled me then. It was like a city unto itself with layers and layers of experience meant only for gay men.

Although the Saint was primarily about dancing, the balcony was the club's site for sex. The sex seemed always beside
the point though. In the world of the Saint, a drugged blowjob was only a moment's rest, a casual hello, and a promise of
something more intense that would have to wait until the
next day. Men were sprawled on top of one another on more
of the gray floor covering, which must surely have been the
filthiest expanse of carpet in existence. I wanted very much
to join them but they were too perfect and too cold. No
denying it, there was a great bitchy meanness to these perfect
specimens. While I shared some traits with these men, like
being white and young, my midwestern, German whiteness

seemed somehow bland in contrast to these descendants of Jews, Greeks, Spaniards, and Italians. Where I was white and soft, they seemed made of marble and mystery. Their bodies, covered only in tight denim or jockstraps, moved with assurance. Even those sprawled on the floor, passed out or overwhelmed, seemed full of grace to me on that one and only night of perfection.

We all hold those perfect moments in our minds like talismans. My perfect moment had nothing to do with romance or bonding. It was, rather, seeing for the first time what gay men could create. I think one of the reasons I rarely went back to the Saint was that I knew instinctively that my special memory would be tarnished through repetition. All the other times I went, I was insanely high, as if I wanted to ensure my awe for the place.

I didn't go to the closing party of the Saint in 1988 that stretched on for days. But I did walk past the front door, the one that faced Second Avenue, on the Monday morning after the club closed for good. Some queen had spraypainted, in enormous letters on the front door, the title of the Saint's signature song by Jimmy Ruffin. "Hold On to My Love."

Evan, who usually interrupts me continually, has been silent on the other end of the phone. I can imagine him in his apartment, smoking furiously, transfixed, with the cell phone pressed against his ear. When he becomes interested in something, his long, lean body stiffens like a pointer that has spotted its bird.

"Fuck. That sounds amazing."

"It was."

Evan clears his throat and I can tell that he feels he's hit pay dirt. "So . . . that's what I'm saying. I want that too. I need that."

"Evan, I had one good night in a disco twenty years ago."

"Come on. What about . . . the Sound Factory, the Palla-dium?" He says these names as if he is reciting a list of the great cathedrals of Europe.

"It was the same at all of them. A lot of snotty queens who never talked to me, let alone had sex with me. I was so high most of the time that I couldn't dance and would just sit on the floor. And, besides, all of that's gone."

"But you were there. That's what I'm saying."

I put down my nail clipper, shift forward in my chair on the patio, and focus. "Evan, I want you to hear this. Once we get to a certain point, we can't go back. Once I started tweak-ing, I never had a good night again. Not one. I couldn't dance, I couldn't be happy; I couldn't do anything but sit in my house paranoid. And neither could you."

"But now I'm sober and why can't I . . ."

"Ok, Evan. You want to go back to that? You wanna see what you're missing?"

"Abso-fucking-lutely. That's what I'm tellin' you, dude."

"You really feel like you need to go?"

"Tellin' you, man, I'm stoked to hit the floor."

"Ok, Resurrection on Saturday night. Let's go."

I can imagine Evan's face falling like a teenager whose dad has decided to go along on his first date. "You're coming with me?"

"If you want to do this, you need to go with somebody sober. So . . . let's go."

There's a silence as Evan assesses his options. Apparently he decides this is the best he's going to get because the next word I hear is "Awesome."

Downtown Los Angeles is in the midst of a revival that is entirely invisible on a Saturday night at midnight as Evan and

I turn onto Broadway. We've brought his car because it's such a disaster—rear view mirrors hanging down, twisted from their brackets, and the front fender duct taped into place—that no one would aspire to steal it. The interior is not in much better condition. The seats are permanently dusted with cigarette ashes and various wires hang out of the dashboard as if it had thrown up. Along Broadway, homeless people are lined up against wire fences, and riot gates have been clamped down to protect storefronts against invasion. The trendy young professionals who are supposedly renovating lofts in the area are nowhere to be seen. Instead, the street gapes open, empty. It could easily serve as a set for the kind of action pic that sends tanker trucks hurtling out of control and cop cars cartwheeling into flaming projectiles.

Broadway is lined with enormous theaters from L.A.'s golden age, much discussed but long forgotten. These gilded palaces now sit empty except for the occasional architectural tour or hungry developer sniffing profit. Evan sees none of this though. His tall frame is bent into the little car's seat and he grips the wheel in anticipation. His shirt has already been discarded and he has dusted his muscled torso with glitter that shimmers, incongruous, in the filthy confines of the car. He looks as if he should be playing Oberon in a college theater production of "Midsummer Night's Dream." The stereo blasts a song that repeats the lyrics, "It's your life . . . love . . . and happiness."

A stream of Evan-clones appears in front of one of the theaters as we pull past a line of taxis to a valet. All the clones are dressed, to the extent that they are dressed, in white. Their sculpted bodies are tan and lithe beneath tight, white shorts or white jeans. The few shirts in evidence are made of filmy, open white gauze that floats open with every movement to reveal rippled abs and bursting pecs. Evan grabs two glossy black tickets from the dash and I can just barely hear him whisper, "Resurrection."

Perversely, I have selected the clothes most likely to make me feel like an alien in this crowd. Dressed in a black T-shirt, tattered jeans and black boots, I clamber out of the car and notice that I look as if I've been rolling around in an ashtray. Brushing at myself like a fussy grandmother, I follow Evan into the hoard of men pressing their hairless, perfect bodies into the ornately carved foyer of the theater. Now that Evan has arrived, all of the awkwardness he displays during the daytime hours falls away. He turns to me, a huge easy smile spreading across his face, and takes my hand, guiding me like a child on the first day of school. He hands the tickets to a security guard talking into a headset, who nods at Evan and looks straight through me. Like a young colt set free in a pasture, Evan pulls me along.

Unlike at the Saint, there is no transition from the outer world into a sacred space. We are immediately through the shallow lobby and into the tropical wetness of male sweat, flashing lights, and throbbing sound. The seats have been removed from the theater and the auditorium has been raised up to the level of a stage that beckons from the far end of the gilded cavern. A huge canvas oval hangs like a cap over the stage, angled back toward the orchestra pit to reveal swimming video projections of shirtless men exactly like those who dance beneath it. Evan pauses for a minute and beams at me. He has transformed under these waves of black light into a faceless, nameless, interchangeably perfect creature. He says something and I can hear nothing of it so I just nod as he pulls me into the sea of flesh.

I'm largely invisible now, cloaked in black, in this swaying mass of white cloth and light brown flesh. Evan moves without self-consciousness, seemingly without thought, into a kind of trance. Hands float up to stroke the soft angles of his muscled body. He neither acknowledges nor dismisses the attention of the men around him. He simply accepts it as his right. The light turns bright and cold with a new crescendo of sound. Evan's back arches, his heart reaching upward into the light with his arms stretched out to the anonymous caresses as he revolves slowly in the adoration. A diva's voice soars out of an array of speakers directly overhead: *"Don't you give up those dreams. Just think of what it means to be a star."*

We enter that strange state of dance that I remember from so many years before, from the days before coke and crystal turned me into a paranoid mess. When I first started dancing regularly in the New York clubs, I would barely drink, let alone do drugs. Dino, never having been much of a dancer, sent me out on my own or with friends and I went without shame because I truly was just going to dance. For someone who had grown up with bland Top 40 radio, the audacity of the music, the twirling drag queens and the shirtless, sweating bodies were enough to propel me through a long night of dancing. Tuesdays and Fridays were my regular dancing nights. On Tuesday nights, I would head to a black club on the then-deserted industrial edges of Chelsea, while Fridays were spent at a tiny, mostly Latin club near the Flatiron Building. Over the course of a year or two, I moved from people giving me a bump of coke or crystal to buying drugs from the dealers working in the clubs. I also moved on from the intimacy of the smaller clubs where I had a regular spot on the floor and would see the same faces week after week, knowing them at least well enough to nod.

When I started to frequent the Sound Factory in the early

nineties, I always arrived with a pocket full of drugs and danced alone in the cavernous space filled with anonymous, changing faces. Dancing had become a pretense to hunt for sex and I left as soon as I could line up the evening's trick. This meant missing the moment in the early morning when the music mellows and the dancers move as one. Even when I did stay, the drugs had ruined dancing for me because I was sure that I was moving in spastic jerks, off the beat, and that everyone was staring at me.

But tonight, the lights and the repetitive beat hypnotize me. Time disappears. Sheets of white light sweep across the floor, across men dressed in white, and I think of how stupid I've been all these years to miss this experience. The wonder I felt twenty years ago at the Saint is still available to me sober and I look guiltily at poor Evan who is so happy here. He looks back at me, in ecstasy, and takes my hands, drawing them up to the ceiling as if to say, "You see?" And I just nod as we sway in the center of these men.

After what seems like hours, I shout into Evan's ear that we should get some water and he nods reluctantly. Moving through the sweaty crowd, their eyes follow mostly Evan but then glance at me, trying to discern our relationship and what that might mean to the possibility of being with Evan. Evan clasps a few men in a quick embrace with whispered assurances, nods, and brief kisses but doesn't stray far from my side. The music has slowed and grown heavier but still the kind of anonymous, soaring soprano associated with house music floats on top, shimmering with promise above the ominous pounding rhythm.

Evan and I lean against a bar, swigging bottles of water, and surveying the expanse of flesh spread out before us. A blond boy runs at full speed into Evan and wraps his wet flesh around Evan's glittering torso. Evan's big arms fold the boy into his chest and their mouths seek one another out. I first try to ignore them but, after a moment, openly gape at their sheer beauty. When they unwrap themselves, Evan looks at me sheepishly and makes an introduction, of which I cannot hear a word, so I just nod and shake the boy's hand. He seems to be made of marble, shorter than Evan but with ridges of muscles moving mysteriously, deeply, under his pale young skin, unmarked by hair. He whispers to Evan now and Evan smiles, shakes his head and shouts something into the boy's ear.

The boy turns to me fully now and the light catches his face. It is more handsome than I anticipated with lines that will mature into true masculinity in a few years. But the light also falls into his eyes and it truly does fall, sucked deep into their blank darkness. His pupils are dilated to the outer rims of the corneas, making his eyes appear flat and dead; dead fish eyes, we call them at the House. The outer edges of his lids twitch with craziness and now I notice his jaw grinding away, little piles of muscle building up and shifting under the perfect cheekbones.

I look at Evan. He is still smiling but looks terrified.

The boy leans in to my ear, putting his arms around my neck and I hear his voice for the first time, hoarse and pumping with breath, "You're with Evan, right? Maybe the three of us can party later?"

There is a sharp smell to the boy that I recognize immediately. It underlies the dull sweaty tones of his scent like bleach poured onto meat. I pull my head back to see Evan, eyes wide with panic, staring at us.

Unwrapping the boy's arms from my neck, I put my hand on his cheek, heaving with grinding jaw muscles, and shout in his ear, "Thanks man but we're not staying that late."

The boy's head whips around to Evan now, seeking a second opinion. Evan just looks away. The boy's face falls into a scowl but, a moment later, the music builds into a bridge to the next song and he looks up at the glowing light display, smiles and simply walks away without another word.

Evan looks relieved but shaky. I don't want this to end badly for him so I smile encouragingly and nod my head toward the dance floor. As we shove past sweaty bodies, I feel disgusted somehow by the accumulation of other men's sweat on me, permeating my shirt, and commingling with my own drenching perspiration. I feel a pair of hands on me and I feel pleased to finally be getting some attention. When I look up, I see two sober smiles. Vidor's massive body is so built up that he seems to be moving around inside of it and his dark hair is plastered down over his face. His boyfriend, whose name I can never remember, wears a similar muscle suit.

Vidor's massive arms encircle me and we are spinning, twirling, and laughing. Without any physical attraction, I am completely in love with his spirit, his outrageous femininity totally out of step with his physical bulk, and an undercurrent of seriousness masked by silly campiness. Suddenly, the dankness of the place feels refreshed.

With his big arms, Vidor moves me away from him like a doll and shakes his big shaggy head, "Girl, you are the last one I thought I'd find here."

"What can I do? Momma had to babysit." I nod toward Evan who is busily gyrating against Vidor's delighted boyfriend. "You know Evan."

Vidor's eyes lick every inch of Evan's supple muscles. "Mmm-hmm."

"Be good. He's only got two months."

"Oh, I'll be very good, honey," Vidor murmurs in my ear before he sandwiches both me and Evan between him and his boyfriend, who forms a sort of back wall of heaving flesh.

I call out to Evan, "I guess you've met these guys. They're sober a long time. Stick with them."

Evan leans into me and gives me a shy little kiss on the cheek, "Thank you . . . for letting me come."

The music explodes and the four of us blow away from one another, our arms raised to the shower of silver strips that descend to the floor. *"Don't forget, don't regret, you're a star."*

As always with me, happiness comes with a tinge of something like grief. The present always reminds me of the past. Nostalgia is such a strange emotion, deepening pleasure by reminding me of something no longer present. Waves of the past roll and break powerfully over the sights and sounds of tonight. As I look over this dance floor, shadows assemble on the periphery, specters of other dance floors and other times. The revolving disco ball is joined by a phantom disco ball that descends from high above, its points of light mingling sadly and slowly with the real illumination. The scrim hanging above the stage shimmers with the image of thousands of boys like Evan. Happy. But my eyes move restlessly above the video images, up to the ceiling. It is a huge dome of blackness, pricked with the light of twinkling stars that slowly, slowly fall from the sky. More shadows are assembling on the edges of the dance floor—fan dancers, leather men, clones with droopy moustaches—and they move into the space between the living men, moving to every other beat in a sad syncopation. I wipe the beads of sweat from my face and realize that they're tears.

I stop dancing. Just standing there still and stupid in the middle of this movement and Vidor's arms are around me, sweeping the tears from my face. "Good or bad?" he asks.

"Sad."

"I know, honey." He glances at Evan who has noticed nothing. "But what can you do?"

"You guys take care of him?"

"Sure, sweetheart." His tongue snakes out of his mouth. "Believe me, you'll regret it. She's a mess."

Vidor nods. "Don't worry. I'll be good."

I move to Evan and kiss his cheek. "I'm going. You stick with these two, okay?"

Evan is shocked but also a little relieved, "You're goin'? You sure?"

"I'm sure. You'll be all right. I'm leaving you with my bodyguards."

Vidor and his boyfriend pull Evan away, encircling him with their G.I. Joe bodies and Vidor shouts out, "Momma's leavin', honey. Now you get to be bad."

Outside the sky is starting to brighten with that sad pink of dawn that is so different from the fiery colors of sunset. The city is utterly deserted. Even the homeless have disappeared into the shelters or beneath whatever shelter they can find in a cardboard box. My ears buzz and hum with the accumulated harm of the speakers and I can still hear the pounding beat from within the theater. As I walk toward a taxi, I know that whatever promise the world inside those walls held for me has been lost. I now belong to the world of morning, not night.

Chapter 6

TINA FOR TONY

It's still raining. The local news calls it a "rain event," and on television a somber looking weather lady paces before images of crumbling canyon walls, collapsing cliffside mansions, families clinging to ropes in flooded rivers, and freeways that are, as always, standing still. Most of these things happen regularly, it's just that this week the cause is rain. The whole city is trembling with a mix of excitement and dread at the thought of weather. Earthquakes, wildfires, and riots have their own particular thrills but they are violent and short-lived. The rain is cumulative and Los Angeles is unsure how to cope with disasters that build rather than explode. This morning the weather lady intoned gravely that the earth was already saturated, and though there was a chance of sun tomorrow, the water would continue to percolate deep in the earth, making hills that had been standing strong for decades deeply unstable. All the earth is liquefying beneath our feet.

I'm thinking of this instead of Pauline's discourse on the difficulties of being a transgendered woman. The residents are huddled deep into the tattered sofas, seeking warmth, as Group grinds on and on. A fire blazes in the hearth across the room but I feel no discernible heat. Pauline, however, shows no sign of being cold, only manic. Though her shoes can't possibly be expensive, they look as if they could be Manalo Blahniks. She has quite shapely legs, covered by nude hose, and she shows them off with a skirt that barely grazes her knees as she sits with her ankles crossed in a ladylike pose. She often refers to her quest to "act like a lady" in the face of the slings and arrows of life as a trans.

I'm filled with superficial, judgmental thoughts as I evaluate her realness. Her lower half is quite successful and even her torso has its comely aspects. Because Pauline must be well into her fifties, the normal male fleshiness of that age mimics a feminine softness that is accentuated by the swelling of her implants. The problem, as always, is with the extremities. Pauline's hands are great fleshy pads that remain intractably male despite her long nails painted in a demure pinkish white. The face is always the ultimate problem for those trans people wishing to pass. Pauline's problems are typical: a forceful jaw, a jutting chin, and features that are generally thicker than those of a woman. Her hair is also problematic. The color of straw, it reaches desperately for her shoulders but, at its ends, grows thin and frayed.

I think of all this as Pauline continues her indictment of the world's wrongs against her. The other residents glance at me, desperate for me to interrupt her. I lean forward, preparing.

"Pauline, let me stop you."

"I'm just trying to be a lady, Patrick, and stop reacting to people but . . ."

"But it's hard and I understand that. But this isn't a transgender support group. You're here because you're an alcoholic and addict."

Pauline's eyes are looking at me but not looking at me.

She has a psych diagnosis but she seems fairly lucid. She re-crosses her legs, "I never really liked to drink."

"So?"

"I'm just saying."

"Pauline, I asked you to read your snapshot."

"I don't know if I'm ready."

"How long have you been here?"

Pauline doesn't answer now but she's been here for two weeks and her snapshot was written days ago. Each resident is directed to write a snapshot of his or her last few days drinking and using. They are to transcribe the experience into the front cover of their *Twelve Steps and Twelve Traditions*, carrying it with them everywhere, so that they are able to refer to it every time they feel like using.

"Pauline, you've spent a half hour describing in general terms how hard it is to be trans. Why won't you take two minutes and tell us how hard it was to be a drug addict?"

"I'd be happy to and thank you for the opportunity," she murmurs and pushes her big coke bottle glasses up on her nose.

Pauline opens her *Twelve and Twelve* and begins to describe her last night using. As I assumed, Pauline was a tweaker, preferring to slam it straight into her veins if possible. Like many trannies, she worked as a prostitute to support herself and her habit. In this case, she was not only feeding her habit but also providing for her boyfriend/pimp, a paraplegic Vietnam vet in San Diego. Every evening, he would send Pauline out to trawl the streets bordering the naval base for soldiers looking for a good blowjob. With a certain pride, she carefully details the sheer blouse and micro-mini she wore that last night. She describes every feature of her extra tall white boots with the stiletto heels that she pulled on before leaving the house. ("They always gave my pinkie toe a big blister but they made my legs look fierce.") The ocean breeze must have been cold but she'd hit the meth pipe before she went out and was feeling fine. Within a block Pauline was picked up by an old guy who "gives me forty for a bj." It's a productive night and Pauline has a series of customers who are eager for her fellatio talents. A few also fuck her ass in the back seats of their cars or in cheap motels that rent rooms by the hour near the base.

Most of her earnings are later smoked at her dealer's house, and at dawn she finds herself near the ocean, flashing her tits at men to try and get a few last takers. It's not even that she wanted to make more money at that point. "I just needed a little more of . . . you know."

"A little more what?" I ask her. "More crystal?"

"More of that . . . feeling."

"What kind of feeling?"

Pauline's face is blank behind a thick mask of makeup. "That feeling like . . . night."

Although I know night is not an emotion, I can only nod in recognition. Pleased not to be challenged on something, Pauline launches back into her story. Finally, near seven in the morning, with the sun burning off the fog, she returned home to her paraplegic boyfriend with the last of the tweak and a few dollars. That morning, Pauline explains, passed like most others. She blew her boyfriend although neither one of them could get it up and then in the afternoon passed out until it was time to hit the streets again.

Pauline has recounted these experiences with all the passion of a grocery list. She blinks her eyes, looking to either side for reaction and then decides to just sit in the silence.

"How many years did that go on for?"

"Oh, Patrick, that was years and years. Ten at least."

"OK. So, Pauline, that was pretty honest."

Pauline's not falling for this easy compliment from me but feels compelled to say, "Thank you. I did my best."

"I don't think you did. You didn't say what you felt about all that. What do you feel?"

Her eyes are unfocused again and I think she almost uses her mental illness as a refuge. She doesn't come back so I ask again, "Pauline, you turned tricks every night to get more crystal. You let anybody fuck you for a few bucks. How does that feel?"

"I never charged less than forty, Patrick."

The other residents snicker but I don't want her to wiggle away. "OK, good for you. You were a highly paid prostitute. How does that make you feel?"

She draws herself up now and assumes a librarian attitude. "Well . . . I feel very sorry about that but now I'm here and trying to be a lady and take responsibility for my life."

"What? You feel sorry and now you're trying to be a lady?" This is the part that makes me uncomfortable. The part when I can see how easy it is to identify bullshit and it makes me wonder if most of what I say is bullshit too. Still, it's why I'm here so I continue. "This isn't a finishing school for young ladies. You're a burned-out, junkie whore who got too old to turn tricks and ended up in a recovery house. How does that make you feel?"

Pauline's sticking with her tactic and she just crosses her legs. "You know it's hard out there for a woman like me and I did what I had to do."

"Oh, so you're an addict because it's hard to be a transsexual?"

She's having a harder time sticking to her image of a proper lady now but she flips her hair back and collects herself. "I certainly never did these things before . . . the people out there . . ."

"You never drank and used before you changed gen-ders?"

"I didn't say that."

"So what are you saying?"

"I'm saying . . ." She's mad now but she won't let loose with the stream of invective that is clearly building up in her. "I'm saying, Patrick, that it's hard."

"You know what, honey, it's hard for all of us. We all had something happen to us that we used as an excuse to get loaded. And you know what the problem is, Pauline?" She's picking at one of her chipped fingernails now. "The problem is that it's still gonna be hard when you get out of here. People are still gonna be assholes to you. So if you don't start dealing with the fact that you're an addict, regardless of the trans thing, what are your options except to use again?"

Judy and I have a debriefing session everyday after Group. After I recount Pauline's progress, or lack thereof, Judy sticks a pen in her mouth and has a good chew. She's not looking at me and not looking away from me. She's just mulling it over.

I begin to worry that I'm going to get Pauline kicked out of the House so I interrupt Judy's prolonged silence, "It's not like I think she can't make progress. It's just gonna take a while longer."

Judy's eyes fasten on to me and a little shiver runs through my body. She takes the well-worn pen from her mouth and sticks it behind her ear. "Oh, I'm not worried about Pauline. She's right on schedule. Deluded and victimized."

"So . . . what're you thinkin' about?"

Judy's voice leaps an octave, which is usually an indicator that she knows exactly what's going on. "You, honey. I'm a little concerned about you."

"Me?"

"Remember we talked about how it can bring up stuff working here?"

"Yeah. And it has. Like with Ding-Dong."

"Mmm-hmm."

"And it's hard. Most days I leave I feel like a truck ran over me."

Judy's voice moves a few keys higher as she squeaks out, "When's the last time you went to a meeting?"

So now I'm busted and I've been around long enough to just admit it. "Few weeks ago."

Judy gives me a big smile. "A few weeks ago? You must be gettin' a little twitchy."

"Does it show?"

"Oh, yeah, honey."

"I'm here all day and then I feel like I've done my thing. Last thing I want at night is . . ."

"Not the same thing. This is work. You're focused on other people and their shit. At night, you need to focus on yours. Especially when you're doing this kind of work."

"I guess I know what I'm doin' tonight."

Judy's already out of her chair and onto her next task. Her voice pipes behind me. "Good."

My route home takes me along Santa Monica Boulevard and the quickly gentrifying warehouses of lower Hollywood. Though it's only late afternoon, a few boys walk the boulevard between La Brea and Highland. A few are impossibly beautiful, new to the street, freshness evident in every one of the calculatedly casual moves. John Rechy is one of my great heroes and I love what he says about prostituting himself, "Sometimes after a night of hustling and then moving to dark cruising

alleyways, I come home and literally think of nothing but sui-
cide. Other times, when I'm caught in it, I think:'Jesus, God,
this is the most exciting thing in the world.' " And I can see
both sides of it in these boys.The young, cute ones are jazzed
on the power of it.They are amped up by the physical mani-
festations of desire: prices negotiated, bills passed, and drugs
bought to keep it going.

Then there are the others. Pauline's right on one level.
The trannies have it hard cause they're hated on both sides.
Here comes a black "girl" with a pink leatherette mini, orange tube top, and nappy hair. She must be well over two
hundred pounds. I can almost hear her snappin' as she walks
and a few gay boys, not hustlers, cross the street, snickering
and shaking their heads. A sexy Mexican guy pulls up next to
her now and she waves to him with a little wiggle of her fingers, sashaying over to his car, and purposefully sticking her
ass as far up in the air as possible when she leans into the passenger window. She'll probably suck him for a twenty. Afterward, he might give her a little small talk or, if he thinks too
much about her tucked cock, beat the shit out of her. Some
of the trannies can't get the money together to pay for real
titties so they just have paraffin shot in that hardens and slips.
Waking up with tits in their armpits, they just shove the hard
lump back on top of their chests and hit the streets. What's a
girl to do?

Just as sad are the burned-out, too-old gay boys. Boys in
name only, these guys are hitting forty and still trying to make
it work. This isn't an abstract thought; Lewis is standing on
the next corner, trying to drape himself alluringly over a bench
at the bus stop. If he seemed skeletal when I last saw him at
the House, he seems dead now. Nothing moves except his
eyes and occasionally, slowly, like a lizard, his tongue emerges to

run along his cracked lips. I turn the corner before he can see me.

I got to the meeting early tonight. I hate to be early because I don't know what to do with myself. So I hesitated at the door, thinking I might walk around the block or go for coffee. Then I saw Tony. Not only were his eyebrows completely gone, there were jagged scabs running across his brow where I suspected he had taken tweezers to his flesh, trying to extract the hairs before they surfaced. He was sitting in the corner, crying quietly. It was early and the room was empty except for his fleshy little body pushed against the wall. He looked up at me briefly and then seemed to fold up on himself.

Now I'm sitting with Tony and he's squeezing my hand like it's an exercise ball. I don't know him well and am, frankly, repulsed by his eyebrow thing. I'm not thrilled with the idea of touching his hand, which looks clean but feels slightly sticky. Tony is dressed all in white as if he has just been laundered. His hair looks as if it has been hacked at with dull scissors, with dull yellow hunks of it hanging across his face. But the strange thing is the absence of Angie, his constant companion.

I extricate my now soaking wet hand and ask, "Where's Angie, honey?"

A noise whistles out of Tony's throat that sounds like something from an exorcism. His face reddens as he stumbles to his feet, "Is she . . . that . . . I . . . I . . ."

I grab Tony's hand again and pull him back down to the seat. With the comfort of my hand in his, he settles back into the chair. "She's not here, sweetheart. I was just asking."

Tony looks at me with the saddest eyes I've ever seen. He points in no particular direction, whispers "Angie," and begins to cry again.

"What happened, Tony?"

For the next thirty minutes, as people slowly fill the seats in the meeting hall, Tony recounts for me his weekend in the desert. It seems that Angie had disappeared a few weeks ago and Tony had been frantically searching for her. Finally, he ran into a former drug buddy who said that Angie had resurfaced in her old trailer outside of Desert Hot Springs and was cooking again. Tony continued to call Angie's cell and, after another few days with no contact, got in his car.

I could imagine Tony, in his little wreck of a Honda Civic with no air-conditioning, hoping that it would make it up the long hills past Chino on the 10 freeway, past the car dealerships, and the Cabazon Outlet Mall. He must have held his breath until the car finally plunged down past the mountains and into the desert surrounding Palm Springs. Tony's voice is all wheezing breath punctuated by strange gulps and twitching eyes. He's not talking to me as much as spitting out his monologue and I know that I'm interchangeable with anyone else who would listen.

Tony must have known somewhere deep inside that he wasn't looking to help Angie but, rather, get high. After all, he knew she was cooking again but he went anyway and went alone. When he reached the wasted expanse of scrub outside Desert Hot Springs, I'm sure he was already grinding his teeth and probably felt like he needed to take a shit.

Everything Tony describes is vividly real to me because I've seen many pictures of meth labs on the net and I have to admit they fascinate me. They all have certain characteristics. Meth labs are never set up in solid houses and they are always isolated. By their nature, they are suited to disposable structures like trailers and prefab houses—places easily destroyed and abandoned. There can be nothing close because of the odor of chemicals. That's what Tony describes first: a sharp puff of ammonia odor as soon as he opened the car door in front of Angie's old trailer. He knew then what would happen and he could have turned but he was transfixed. I realize that Tony's story is triggering me but I stay here, leaning towards him, asking him questions, and prompting him to give details. This isn't for him, I realize, because I feel high listening to him and I like it.

Tony gives a long dissertation on the smell of the lab. It came not just from the trailer, with its windows closed tight and faded yellow shades drawn down. The smell, he said, came from everywhere. Angie must have been busy because there were some burn pits where she'd been getting rid of the by-products rather than having to take them to the town dump. The solids had been burned in shallow little graves and nearby were pools of red where she'd poured the liquids down into the sand. The earth had soaked up the gallons of sticky toxicity, pulling it down into the water supply. The whole desert must be toxic by now from cookers pouring their waste down into the aquifer that feeds the elegant pools and fountains of Palm Springs. Now, instead of water, meth waste percolates through the sand. All of the desert must be tweaked. There was an article in the Los Angeles *Times* the other day explaining that the cavernous aquifer under Palm Springs, providing what had once seemed like a limitless supply of water, had been emptied. Palm Springs and the surrounding towns now sit on a fragile crust of earth, sinkholes waiting to open.

Tony knew better than to simply open the front door of the trailer or even knock. Angie always kept a wide variety of shotguns in her lab when she was cooking because her hands were too shaky to depend on a handgun that required aiming. The shotgun could just be sprayed in the general direction of an intruder. Tony had been with Angie on long runs and watched her booby trap the front doors and windows with shotguns hung high, focused down, cocked, and attached to a taut string waiting to trigger death. Potential invaders ranged from cops to angry dealers to other cookers who'd decided it was easier to steal than manufacture. Angie's caution was part tweaker paranoia and part common sense as the Hell's Angels had recently been hunting down "Beavis and Butthead shops" like Angie's and burning them to the ground or worse.

In any case, Angie knew Tony was there. He didn't need to knock or call. He just needed to wait her out. Tony had seen one of the shades move ever so slightly when he got out of the car. Knowing he wasn't going away, Angie must have been calculating the relative risks and benefits of letting him in. It was probably pretty lonely, even for a tweaker, out there in the desert. On the other hand, Angie knew Tony well enough to be aware that he was a vacuum that could easily snort up her profits and, God knows, he never had any money to actually buy. Tony was pretty much a losing proposition for her.

Tony couldn't go too close to the door in any case because Angie had acquired her usual pit bull, which was chained to a spike near the entrance to the trailer. The dog alternately lunged to the limit of its chain, snarling, and collapsed on the hot dusty yard exhausted. Angie didn't much bother to feed her dogs, preferring them hungry and mad, knowing that she could always get another if the current one finally succumbed to the beating desert sun.

Tony had no interest in describing his emotions or looking back at the decisions he made toward using. He was fascinated by the exterior facts of the scene as if they held some essential truth. This had always been true of Tony. He could recount the most horrendous experiences, emotionless, as if he were reading a novel. While he couldn't describe his decision to sit on the ground and wait out Angie, he could describe the red phosphorous stains on the ground. He told me how the wind came up and the rest of the world seemed to disappear in the haze of dust. It was only Tony and Angie, sitting in the desert, waiting for each other as the pit bull howled mournfully.

Tony wasn't sure if it was ten minutes or more like an hour but, finally, the front door opened. The pit bull whimpered and cowered as Angie appeared, preceded by her usual hacking cough. She pulled on a pair of huge sunglasses and stared at Tony for a long while. Angie didn't invite him in, just muttered, "Can't smoke in here," before disappearing back into the trailer. She left the door open and Tony knew that was as much of an invitation as he was likely to get.

Tony crept past the pit bull that still cowered but growled deep in his throat as Tony put his foot on the first step. Angie's voice shot out of the trailer, "Ciera la boca o te parto la madre!" The dog whined and pulled both its ass and head toward the sand like a potato bug curling into itself for protection.

Although I've seen many photos of meth labs, it was the thought of Tony actually in one that made his descriptions of the lab horrifying and fascinating to me. In photos, the tangles of tubing running between glass jars and bowls remain abstractions, almost like some demented sculptural installation. But when I look at Tony and think of him standing in the midst of all that poison, it becomes real. Angie always ran a fairly clean shop but there's no way to have that much toxic shit in a trailer and not create chaos. She'd apparently stashed most of her equipment in a storage locker when she got clean the last time and so was able to reassemble a pretty high-end lab. From the start, Angie'd never been interested in fucking around with some lab thrown together in the trunk of her car. Instead of jam jars and measuring cups, she'd gone to Kmart and invested in Visionware bowls that could take both high heat and cold. She'd also been smart enough to hook up with a Sudafed wholesaler, knowing that sooner or later, it would be restricted. When she decided to go back into business, Angie already had the basic ingredients of the trade, waiting and combustible, in the storage locker. She had everything but the pH strips to test acidity and she knew she could make those out of red cabbage if she had to.

Tony's voice lowers with awe as he recites the ingredients and process for cooking meth. I try to make him get to the point but instead he revels in the sick recipe for cooking Tina. Angie, like most cookers now, uses the Nazi method. It's not just a name or a myth but the actual process developed by the Nazis to produce the extraordinarily powerful crank that kept Hitler wired and crazy enough to kill millions. One of Tony's eyes twitches and pulses as he stammers out the alchemical process that takes poison and transforms it into evil magic.

There were empty boxes of Sudafed everywhere in the trailer. All day, all night, Angie would crush thousands of pills and soak them in denatured alcohol to make an acidic liquid that would be boiled on her tiny stove. The pseudoephedrine was filtered, frozen, and boiled again until she finally dried it using a hair dryer, revealing the basic ingredient for the tweak. Next came the iodine. She'd always found getting it was a pain in the ass so she'd knocked-off a farm supply store a couple of years ago and stashed away gallons of iodine tincture. Phosphorus was another story. Easier to come by and ostensibly legal, red phosphorous production was a perfect tweaker project involving lots of chemicals, time, and obsessive behavior.

The phosphorous production necessitated cutting the strike pads from hundreds and hundreds of matchbooks, soaking them in acetone, scraping the phosphorous from the pads, rinsing, drying and grinding it to produce the necessary red powder.

Tony recounts the full recipe by heart, obsessively listing each ingredient and strange step. He moves on to the chemicals that are more readily available and more likely to kill you. Sulfuric acid. Ammonia. Open bubbling beakers of the shit surrounded by the necessary flames of burners.

When we would go for coffee after meetings, Angie often talked about her days as a cooker. In the past, Angie had never put up with crazy tweaker shit lying everywhere in the lab because she knew it was easy to knock over a beaker of acid or ammonia and blow herself all the way to hell. But the days of caution had apparently passed. Tony tells me with disgust that the floor of her trailer was covered with little piles of obsessively sorted clothes, newspapers, and a selection of Narcotics Anonymous books. Tony took the books to be a hopeful sign of her continued willingness. As he suspected, there were also assorted shotguns positioned by every window and, of course, the front door. A laptop computer and cell phone sat incongruously amongst the trash—slick, shiny and new tools amidst the squalor.

When I ask Tony about Angie's health, he tells me that her hands and neck are now stained red from either the phosphorous or the coating on the Sudafeds. Angie had always been rail-thin and she'd gotten thinner during her time in the desert. Apparently, her fingernails had become as suspicious as her eyelashes because most of them were gone as well.

Angie hadn't offered Tony any tweak. Even in her state, she probably couldn't deal with the guilt of getting Tony high. But it was understood that it was his for the taking and he lasted no more than five minutes in the trailer before he had snorted enough Tina to keep him up for a week. The problem was that there was never enough Tina for Tony. He was like a dog in a room full of hamburger.

Angie made it clear that Tony was leaving in the morning. She might have felt guilty but she more likely understood that their friendship, so touching in sobriety, would interfere with her business and that could not happen. She knew that a fried queen like Tony was not going to be of any use to her, certainly not in cooking with his shaky hands. He couldn't even sell on the streets. Angie had been around long enough to know that, after a few days tweaked out, Tony would either be leading the cops or boys from one of the gangs back to her trailer. Still, there must have been some comfort in having him there because she told him that he could stay the night.

They spent that night watching TV. Tony kept one eye on the TV and another on the small mound of crystal that Angie had laid out, clearly indicating the amount she was willing to offer. All tweakers have their obsessive behaviors. For most gay men, it's sex. But Tony found that he was no longer much of a draw and his cock rarely worked anyway. He stopped his story, drew in a deep breath, and whispered, "Girl, I ain't cum in years." So instead he channeled his energy into plucking and watching reruns on *Nick-At-Nite*. Tony can, and will if allowed, recite the plots of every episode of *Bewitched*. He finds everything about it fascinating and can deliver a compelling thesis on why the generally creepy first Darrin was hotter than the second. Unfortunately, *Bewitched* is so powerful to Tony that it sends him off into a bit of psychosis as he tells me his story. Suddenly, Angie and the trailer disappear in the details of an episode in which Samantha's favorite tree, a weeping willow, is sick. A spell cast by Dr. Bombay to restore the tree's health instead has the effect of making Samantha "weep." And, in the telling, Tony begins to weep himself.

I let Tony cry for a bit, muttering about Samantha and her tree. He is shaking now, almost like he is in shock. I decide to try to pull him back in. "Tony . . . what happened to Angie? She still out there?"

Tony freezes for a moment and then begins to pick at the scab on his forehead that was formerly an eyebrow. A little blood begins to ooze from it and I grab his hand. "You're hurting yourself, Tony. Stop. What happened to Angie?"

Tony looks around the room and, realizing that it is now mostly filled, pulls his chair even closer to the wall. "She went out to check and that's when it happened."

"Check what?"

"That's when it happened."

"What happened?"

"She's real mad at me."

"What'd you do? You steal some tweak?"

Tony zooms into focus suddenly. This is the most disturbing part of crystal insanity. It's not continuous. Suddenly, Tony pulls himself up in the chair and leans toward me, entirely lucid. "I wanted to. You know . . . course I'd done what she laid out. I had some and I wanted some more and she went outside so I thought . . . fuck, I thought . . . she's cookin' in here, so how hard can it be to find some more."

"She catch you?"

Tony is still with me mentally but his body is starting to shake again. Violently. "Didn't find no more. I was looking around the . . . whatever it is . . . the tubes and shit. Moving some stuff and it was hot and . . . I touched that glass and . . . but no . . . no fire . . . just . . . I . . ."

Tony stops there. He closes his eyes, trying to either see or not see.

"Tony, you've been through this before. You know you're just gonna have to get through these first few days . . ."

A sound somewhere between groaning and humming rises out of Tony's throat as he rocks back and forth on the cheap plastic chair. It groans along with Tony, threatening to snap from the violent motion of his body.

He's shaking so badly that I think maybe I should get some help but I'm afraid he'll bolt. I stand up next to him and say, very softly, "Tony . . . honey, maybe we should walk a little bit."

I touch him on the shoulder and his arm shoots out, stiff and shaking, to hold me away. He is wearing a loose, long-sleeved T-shirt and it slides back on his out-stretched arm.

"Oh, my God." It's all I can say as I look at his arm. Tony opens his eyes slowly now and looks at his arm, calmly, curiously. He pulls the sleeve farther back to reveal his flesh. It has been burned, but not by fire. There is a kind of deep red swirl that wraps around the top of his forearm and then spreads down towards the wrist. His skin looks cauterized from what must have been one of Angie's acids.

"Oh shit, honey. We need to get you to the hospital."

Tony's body stops shaking. He stands suddenly and declaims in a loud voice, to no one in particular, "I'm speaking to Tina now. I'm talking to her directly. Tina, you lifted me up and then you let me down."

Several other guys from the meeting have walked over to us. Everyone is silent now. Just waiting.

"Tony, let's go. We need to . . ."

So quickly that I don't even see him move, Tony is out of the room. We all scramble after him but, when we get to the door, Tony is already halfway down the block, running as fast as he can. Just before he turns the corner, he flings his arm up into the air, as if he's waving, and disappears.

Chapter 7

HEAD DOWN

I have a chance to go to New York on a writing assignment and, for some reason, it feels like a terrible mistake. When I first moved to Los Angeles, I would return to New York now and then but I haven't been back in a few years. Much of the sleazy, dirty New York I loved is gone but the city still has a powerful hold on me because I find ghosts standing on every street corner there.

I'm only going for a few days but I'm using the trip as an excuse to stop working at the House. Everything that Judy has directed me to do so that I can deal with the emotional consequences of working there, I've ignored. I haven't gone to more meetings or kept a journal or even taken the time to really examine why I feel so fucked up. I sit in Group every morning pushing and pushing the residents to be honest when I feel like my sobriety is brittle and dry at the moment. Watching them struggle makes it impossible to ignore my own precarious position. I just want to run.

It's decided and I'm going to New York. On the outside, I can explain it as a job, or at least an opportunity. Yet I know that something deeper is at work and I feel like I'm on the cusp of some great and terrible change. There is a burning in my stomach that intensifies through each day until, lying in bed at night, I begin coughing and choking on sharp bile. My mother tells me that it is acid reflux but that sounds entirely too mundane and I think that surely I'm too young to be sharing diseases with my mother.

Still, something is keeping me sober despite my best efforts to head down another path. That something is, of course, my "higher power." Those two words that have made millions of newcomers to A.A. cringe because of their religious connotation and their sheer geekiness. It's one thing to wallow in our druggy war stories but quite another to start praying.

I never had a problem with the idea of a higher power or even God. As a child, my parents couldn't have been less interested in attending church so I went on my own. I worked the religious circuit in Cherokee, Iowa, moving from the First Church of Christ, to Grace Baptist, to Immaculate Conception. There was no particular event to draw me to any of them but I do remember sitting in each church and waiting for something to happen. It never did until I got sober.

My higher power has changed throughout my sobriety. When I first got sober, I prayed to Dino and was able to feel him around me. After a few years, I felt that he had moved on to wherever he was going. Much like Zelma, I was sleeping one night and dreamed of my dead husband. In the dream Dino walked up to a door and opened it. When he opened that door, I heard myself gasp, and felt something like water pouring over me. I woke up weeping and never felt Dino's presence again.

I moved to Venice Beach and started praying to the ocean, taking long walks just feeling the depth and immensity of the water beside me. Almost every night I would walk out on the Venice Pier at sunset. It stretched before me like a long-handled

frying pan, as strong and graceful as anything made from concrete could be. Almost every night it drew me down its length,
a highway out into the ocean. The sun would already have
sunk below the mountains as I walked out onto the pier. The
world was silhouetted black against the water. Surfers rode
alongside the pier catching modest swells, weaving their boards
in between the pilings before rising up in triumph one last
time, and then sinking languidly back down into the water.
Seagulls flew in perfect formation, gliding parentheses, so
compelling in their unity. Most nights I got there in time to
see the path of gold that the sun formed on the water. Where
the waves broke, the path would be fractured into a thousand
arteries but, as it continued out over the water, the reflection
would gradually consolidate into a gleaming, golden line. When
the sun sank below the horizon, the water reflected the red,
gold, blue, and white clouds in the sky. Each night this revelation of nature was repeated, drawing me to live there and
witness it over and over again. In those moments, I felt God.

There is an enormous circular platform at the end of the
Venice Pier that smells of fish and beer and, sometimes, piss.
Each night, I would walk to the center of it where a small
bronze plaque had been imbedded in the platform. As I ran
my toes over the worn letters of the inscription, I would look
out. Look to the mountains on my right, slowly dipping down
from the Palisades to Malibu and Point Magu. Look to the
left, where the airport shot out jet after jet like artillery fire.
And look, finally, out over the ocean to the horizon where I
knew that the water was miles deep and moved with mysterious creatures. I would stand there, breathing the moist air
deep inside me, and pray that my life would change. I prayed
that my old life would be ripped away from me. As I stood

there, I would trace my toe slowly over the letters on the plaque, reading them as if they were Braille: "Center of the Universe."

But again, after a few years, I moved on. Los Angeles contains a vast spiritual life that is hidden from outsiders and, since moving here, I've been a seeker. I've sat in Indian sweat lodges that were held in backyards of suburban track homes. I've attended yoga classes led by a woman who grew up in New Jersey but now wears a white turban and goes by an Indian name. I've been taken to Bel Air mansions where Hollywood wives sat in a circle around a Kabbalah master asking questions about real estate. And, though I sometimes ridiculed these experiences, I gained something from each of them.

One of my great spiritual adventures was a weekend workshop called the Body Electric that took place in a community center at the base of the Angeles National Forest. The Body Electric morphed out of the radical faerie movement in which gay men dropped out of society during the '60s and sought out a natural spiritual life in rural communes. Now gay faeries are figures of fun, their earthy drag obscuring a strong anti-assimilationist creed built on Marxism and feminism. In the deep woods, they developed rituals that would connect them to the power of nature and their forefathers. Part Native American, part horny group-grope, these rituals are easily dismissed when one sees pictures of men named Persimmon or Cupcake in long dresses and wild hair dancing through the fields or participating in obscure rituals such as saline hypnotherapy.

When I entered the room where the Body Electric was held, I was three or four years sober and deeply tired of nights spent in bathhouses. Twenty men sat in a circle in the room and were addressed by a tall, thin leader with long brown hair. I don't recall whether he really explained the purpose of the weekend or if I understood fully why I was there but, in retrospect, I know that the weekend was designed to help me see worth in other gay men, whether I was attracted to them or not. The first day of the Body Electric was horrifying, including a long ritual during which we got naked and learned how to masturbate one another. We were told not to cum over the course of the weekend and, though the day's masturbation lessons had repulsed me, they had also left me rather horny. That night, I went home feeling disgusted and vowing not to return the next morning. However, my fundamental cheapness reminded me that I had spent several hundred dollars to register for the workshop and I wanted my money's worth.

It is very difficult to describe what happened on the second day of the Body Electric but I remain convinced that the experience ranks alongside my sobriety and being arrested in the streets of New York during ACT UP demonstrations as one of the great healing rituals of my life. All of the shame and awkwardness of the first day dropped away during a long ritual in which two men would massage and pleasure a third person, not to the point of orgasm but rather to a sort of clenched intensity, carefully timed to the music thundering through the space. The two men massaging me looked like Santa Claus and an aged rabbi, but there was something so sweet and gentle about them that I felt entirely content being with them. Their hands traveled over my body, using the techniques we had learned before along with a few that they had clearly acquired elsewhere. At the apex of sexual pleasure, I was told to tense my body and hold my contracted muscles as tightly as possible. After a few moments, the leader called out, "Release." My body fell back down onto the massage table, the hands of my brothers lifted away from my body and, for a few moments at least, I was free and happy. Stars zoomed past my eyes and I felt myself float up and out of my body. I remember weeping at the thought of leaving those men whom I had found repulsive only the day before.

I've had other such experiences in even stranger environments. One weekend I found myself sitting in a convention center with thousands of other seekers spread out in front of an ethereal Indian guru. For two days, we chanted and meditated. My brain had been filled with chemicals for so many years that it was not all that difficult for me to hallucinate. So I was not shocked to have an intense vision that brought me to my next higher power—the Indian god Ganesh.

Sitting in the hall chanting with the guru and the other devotees, I felt something akin to the rushing sensation I'd felt the last time I dreamed about Dino. Suddenly I was not in the convention center but in the ocean. The sea was filled with light. I was far down, at the point where one can no longer see the golden ceiling of the surface. I was far down, cradled in the warm embrace of the liquid world. The sea's inky depths were hung with curtains of light. They extended up to where I knew the surface undulated with wave after coursing wave. The light emanated from everywhere, nowhere. It washed over me, moving to a slow rhythm. The light had mass and the water moved with it, currents shifting and dancing in the light's song. The world rocked back and forth.

"Come, come," the light sang to me, beckoning to me with long, blue-white arms. I breathed liquid. I gave way to the slowly shifting pressure and opened my lungs, letting myself become one with the water, connected. As the water moved, so did I. I had no fear of the black chasm below me. "I know you," a woman's voice sang from far away, "open your eyes." I began to sink down into the cushion of blackness and, as my mind quieted, I saw lights twinkling in the depths. There were stars in the ocean, as remote and distant as in the sky. I decided to leave the safe depth, too close to the dry world that I had known. I wanted nothing but the deep blue sweep of light leading to blackness filled with distant stars. "Come," she said with complete understanding, "it's time."

I flew toward the stars, twinkling in the darkness below, and felt a gathering of energy in and around me. The woman's voice became a plaintive cry without cessation. It was lodged in the base of my spine, throbbing, "Open your eyes, your eyes, your eyes."

I came to a field of sea grass, moving like wheat in the wind. Blue-white fronds billowed in unison, silver rippling over their surface. Moving forward, the grass stroked my legs and groin. I felt the grass moving, alive. I breathed and listened to the song of the woman's voice, called out to it with moans and clicks in my throat. Miles of water rose above me and its weight was a comfort.

I sat cross-legged, my hands on my thighs with the thumb and forefinger touching. Sitting in the same position across from me was a brightly colored elephant. His trunk was curled and pointing upwards, bubbles percolating from it. His black eyes with long lashes watched me intently, never blinking. The elephant's face was chalky white but his body was a garish pink, gaudy as a street fair. His entire being glittered. In two of his hands, with their painted fingernails, he held flowers. The other two hands extended to me, one held up as if to command me to halt, the other holding a softly shimmering blue pearl. I floated to him, drawn by the beauty of the pearl, and settled my head on his huge foot, staring at the azure light that emanated from the orb.

The elephant's words drowned out the woman's voice as he said, "I have but one thing to tell you." I rubbed his soft rosy foot and waited, breathing slowly. "Part of you must die before the greater part can live."

I looked down at my flesh and it was black, as if burned. As I watched, my body began to stir, covered by thousands of black, flickering butterfly eyes. The blue ocean light washed over the eyes in silence. Then there was no voice, no sound, only momentum without movement. The eyes slowly blinked open and shut, thousands of black butterflies. Each open eye contained a patch of light so severe that I could barely look at it. Yet I gave myself freely, with relief, to the obliterating light. In great waves, the eyes all over my body opened, revealing themselves, water streaming from them. I was this burning thing and, it seemed to me that where there had been only darkness, now there was only light.

Funny how such strange and intense visions later seem delusional, self-induced. I also soon felt that the Indian guru was a false prophet, perhaps even a cult leader. However, I still pray to a gaudy statue of the Indian god Ganesh that sits on my desk, illuminated at all times by three white candles. When I get up in the middle of the night and wander to the kitchen, there is always a moment of comfort when I see the dark eyes of the statue lit by the flickering light of the candles. Ganesh is part elephant and part human in form. He is the patron saint of writers and is said to have wanted to write so badly that he broke off one of his tusks to use as a pen.

But I haven't been writing. I've just been living and listening. I've let myself become lost in the stories of the House's residents. Mostly in Group, I hear lies, and the lies of the residents intertwine with my own lies, building a strong thick screen between me and the rest of the world. Because I now share in their lies, I am deeply drawn into the stories of their endlessly varied degradations. The weeks have slipped past and today is my self-imposed last day here. It's an indicator of how the rest of my life feels that the House represents stability to me at this point. This morning, Judy asked me again to stay and, with the supreme confidence of someone doing the right thing, told me that she was keeping the door open for me. But I'm ending this today and I have no idea why. Well, once again that's a lie. I feel on some level that working in recovery is what I'm supposed to do with my life instead of writing, and that thought has terrified my ego so deeply that I need to run. In the culture of Hollywood that I both dismiss and crave, there is no way to see becoming a therapist or a social worker as a triumph.

Today, the Group is reading the Third Step from *Twelve Steps and Twelve Traditions*. Together, they intone, "Made a decision to turn our will and our lives over to the care of God, as we understood Him." Then, each resident reads a paragraph. As they read, their stories flash in my mind.

Ding-Dong teeters into the room and sits next to me, unable to read, slowly rocking back and forth. My hand rests on his shoulder. He likes this contact and flashes me his big, blind smile. He can navigate the House from memory now but the other residents instinctively steer him past sharp corners and obstructions such as furniture and feet.

Next to Ding-Dong is Damian, a shriveled little black queen in his fifties, who sleeps only with "straight" men. Damian showered these men with gifts, money, and, naturally, drugs. Inevitably, Damian's dates evolved into lurid screaming matches that all too closely resembled the mundane heterosexual couplings that the tricks had sought to escape in the first place. Now Damian sits in a decaying house in Hollywood, pining for the butch realness of these men who took everything. But Damian had managed to scare off few of his tricks. When he disappeared into treatment, the "straight" men realized they missed the drugs and the gay sex. Even now, months later, their numbers continue to flash frequently on Damian's beeper and cell phone, taken from him when he entered the House but on view in Judy's office. One of the hungry heterosexuals finally tracked down Damian after asking around on the street and he calls the payphone in the lobby of the House every few days. Damian has been instructed not to take the calls but he continues to circle around the payphone at noon when he knows that his man will be on lunch break and cruising the streets around Santa Monica and Highland, looking for a little attention.

Marlon, on the other hand, was one of those men Damian would have happily serviced out there on the streets. He swaggers around the House in low-hanging jeans and a wife-beater, his gang tattoos running up arms that were once beefy but are now just sinew, eaten away by his relentless appetite for crystal. I find him wildly sexy, adding another secret to the heavy bag that I drag around. Judy bought him a conservative buttoned-down shirt and khaki pants last week, which he hates. After hours of cajoling, he revealed why he is so invested in the masculine thug look. It seems that Marlon also had a "straight" boyfriend who used to send him out to the streets to earn. He was unhappy with Marlon's nightly take so decided to test Marlon's appeal as a trannie. The boyfriend sent Marlon out in full drag splendor and, after no more than an hour, Marlon was sitting on the curb of Santa Monica Boulevard in front of Shakey's Pizza, with his hands cuffed behind his back. The cops had pulled off his wig and Marlon's face was streaked with mascara, running with his tears. After a full night in jail, still in the cheap sheath dress he had donned for work, Marlon vowed never to turn fem again and reverted to his Cholo look. Today, he still hangs onto a vestige of the look with the khakis worn long and the dress shirt worn open to reveal a wife-beater underneath.

There are two women of the biological variety in the room today. Missy resembles a turtle with her head pulled back into her shoulders and her face collapsed into a pockmarked mask from years of shooting smack and meth. Missy specialized in washing checks to support her habit. She is the dark figure who roots through your trash at four in the morning, expertly sorting through the coffee grounds and orange peels to extract a cancelled check you thought was hidden so deep in the garbage bag it would never be found. She is the casual stroller in your neighborhood who deftly grabs the electric bill you've paid and left hanging out of the mailbox for the postman. With her own special blend of acetone, bleach, and typewriter correction fluid, she removes the payee and amount before drying the check with a hair dryer. As carefully as a diamond carver, Missy would iron any warping out of the check and then rewrite it to herself for thousands of dollars. When she was at the top of her game, Missy would load up a stolen car with a laptop, portable printer, and a laminating press to produce IDs that allowed quick conversion of the checks into untraceable cash. This is her fifth time in the House and, as always, she's shown up with her dog and only long-term relationship, Peanut. Peanut is irretrievably filthy. After ten years of living on the streets with Missy, he has become so stained that he simply will not come clean. At this point, he considers the House to be his home and wanders through Group, one ear permanently drooping over his little Schnauzer face and a snaggletooth sticking straight out. The residents reach reflexively for Peanut, dragging the stinky dog up into their laps and burying their faces in his matted fur like the catatonic residents of nursing homes who respond only to the touch of an animal.

Missy usually arrives for rehab straight from another stint in prison but she was not caught washing checks this time. Instead, she freaked out after a three-day run on some tweak and grabbed Peanut, trying to hold him so close to her that he began to suffocate. The dog bit her as delicately as it could but it still set her off and she kicked the poor flea-bitten thing until it was nearly dead. Now, Missy can barely look at Peanut as he drags himself around after her, a constant reminder of the fact that she harmed a soul that was inarguably innocent.

Jason sits next to Missy, cooing softly over Peanut's impassive body, stroking the dog with complete adoration. Jason isn't yet thirty but he's torched his life repeatedly for just a little more tweak. Today, he's happy though, because he's come out to both his parents and his brother. I know that he feels that this admittedly heroic action and the positive response will cure his addiction. For him there is still a long road to understanding that his sexuality was only the first secret to be revealed. Still, it was enormous progress and no one can deny him his day of happiness. Only ten days ago he was sitting in prison after having violated his parole one more time. On his last run, Jason had strolled out of the joint in the white jumpsuit worn by prisoners and headed directly across Los Angeles to his dealer's house. For days, he had slammed tweak and cried, knowing that his parole officer was going to bust him. When he finally called his P.O. and told her that he wanted to stop using drugs, the response had been a direct transfer to the House.

The book is passed to Marie but she just stares at it and shakes her head. Marie is the little girl I saw sitting in the dining room on my first day working here. I've come to know a lot about Marie. Over the weeks her black roots have grown out and only shaggy blond ends, trimmed roughly by another resident, remain. When I first saw Marie close-up, I was shocked by the red streaks running across her face. Judy had explained to me that sometimes tweakers use so heavily that the capillaries burst in their faces and the pores bleed. Marie had literally been sweating blood when she arrived at the House.

Marie is leaving tomorrow to go back to her family, or so she says. I think it is more likely that she will return to Venice Beach where, in a fit of paranoia, she stabbed another tweaker before she ended up here. She made the decision to leave yesterday after she shared with the Group that, desperate for attention as a child, she accused her father of molesting her. I asked her whether he had, in fact, molested her and she sat stone silent. Finally, she started laughing and said no, he hadn't molested her. Then she continued to say that she'd asked her father if she could kiss his penis and he had agreed. I'd asked her again if her father had molested her and she told me no. For nearly an hour, we'd gone back and forth with her laughing, changing her story. And now she sits slumped over the book, having notified the staff this morning that she will be leaving. She doesn't look up but throws the book in Erol's lap.

Erol is perhaps the most fucked-up, arrogant person in the House and, without doubt, the sexiest. He was born in Turkey and his family emigrated to Los Angeles via a ten-year stint in London. His voice is a ladder of accents that hints at his shifting identities. Erol is short, compact, sleek, and covered in black fur with huge arched eyebrows framing pained eyes. He is deeply invested in being a straight man who, out of desperation, abandoned fucking women and now only goes for trannies. My sexuality feels mundane and utterly explainable alongside his complexity. I've spent more than a little time fantasizing about him and his constructed but potent masculinity. Erol's body has regenerated itself in front of my eyes in a month, piling on muscle without exercise.

Erol's presence points out Pauline's absence. When Erol arrived at the House, Pauline promptly decided that he was her new husband. Unfortunately for Pauline, though, Erol's kink for trannies was not strong enough to get past her appearance. She followed Erol around for a week or two, towering over him, until she announced that she was leaving the House.

With an English public school lilt mixing with the burr of his Turkish vowels, Erol reads,

"It is when we try to make our own will conform with God's that we begin to use it rightly. To all of us, this was a most wonderful revelation. Our whole trouble had been the misuse of willpower. We had tried to bombard our problems with it instead of attempting to bring it into agreement with God's intention for us."

After we say the Serenity Prayer together, I ask the Group to sit back down. Judy is standing in the doorway. My voice is already breaking and my eyes feel full.

"This is going to be my last day, you guys."

I'm surprised by their reaction. On most days, the residents look sideways at me, evaluating whether or not I represent a threat. The majority of their hatred is focused on Judy, who is much tougher than I am, but they've hardly been warm and cuddly with me. With the news of my departure, Jason actually gasps a little and Erol begins to cry. It's so typical of my life that I don't know when I've connected with people.

"This was always a temporary thing for me, to fill in until there's a new fulltime counselor. And I . . . I wanna thank all of you."

Each and every one of the residents stands in line to say good-bye to me as I cry like a baby.

★ ★ ★

I'm in Judy's office, still weeping. She just sits and watches. It's the difference between this place and the outside world. Out there, the world reacts to emotion with embarrassment and a friend will rush to say, "Don't cry." Here, all emotion is equal as long as it is honest.

The tears subside and I look at Judy who is slowly nodding her head. After I blow my nose, I offer up what I'm really crying about. "This ended up meaning a lot more to me than I thought it would. In fact, I kind of think I could do it instead of writing. But I'm too scared."

"Too scared of what?"

"My ego. What I think I should be."

Judy isn't a big hugger actually but she gives me one now. "The door's open, honey. Why don't you just accept you don't know what you want? You have no idea how it'll all work out and that's fine."

Most of the residents are eating lunch when I leave. I move quickly past the dining room before they can say anything. As I open the front door, though, Ding-Dong is standing outside, smoking a cigarette. He looks toward me and says, "Who's that?"

"It's Patrick. I'm leaving."

"Oh, OK."

Ding-Dong doesn't look sad or happy, just intent on his cigarette. In the larger scheme of things, my departure is a small event. He turns his face to the sky and blows cigarette smoke upward. "Hey Patrick, is it gonna rain some more?"

I look at the sky. It's filled with huge, puffy clouds, bruised along their edges. "I think so. Yeah."

"Well," Ding-Dong says, tossing his head, "that makes my hair curly."

Looking at Ding-Dong now, smoking and thinking about his hair, he becomes a real person. "Ding-Dong, can I ask you a question?"

"Oh, sure," he says. "I hope it's personal."

"It is. What's your real name?"

Ding-Dong stares at me with his opaque eyes and extends his hand. "Robert Alistair Tompkins." He winks. "But you can call me Bobby."

I shake his hand. "Very nice to meet you, Bobby."

In my first months of sobriety, my sponsor told me to "be good to myself" and I interpreted that as getting as many spa treatments as possible. Facials and manicures seemed the perfect panacea to years of snorting poison and blowing out my liver. Having left the House with my eyes red and puffy, I head to a spot where I've spent many a weepy afternoon.

The Beverly Hot Springs is secreted away behind an ugly stucco façade on Beverly Boulevard in Koreatown. The luxury of the building reveals itself only from the parking lot, where my car is whisked away by a valet. I enter through a set of glass doors into a tall marble atrium with a waterfall rushing down. The sound and smell of water is everywhere in the complex, which is built on a natural alkaline hot springs. The odor of sulfur, eucalyptus, and mint drift heavily through the reception area, distracting me from the hefty charge the Korean woman zips onto my credit card. In early sobriety, most of my income went to paying off my spa bills but I rarely treat myself to a massage here anymore because prices have skyrocketed with the influx of Hollywood agents and actors who have become devoted to the place.

Upstairs, I hand my receipt to a little Mexican man in exchange for some towels and a razor. He then waves me into what looks to be a gym locker-room but with a few slabs of marble added for luxury. I deposit my clothes in a locker and secure the key, mounted on a stretch band around my ankle before walking naked into the spa itself.

It is drizzling again and only a weak light drifts through a skylight, further shadowed by the slowly rotating blades of a fan. The spa is mostly deserted on a weekday afternoon but a few Korean men sit on short concrete stools that look like flat-topped mushrooms in the grooming area. One man intently examines his body, squeezing blemishes and methodically plucking out hairs. A few obviously gay men lounge naked in plastic chairs near the main pool. Two of them are marked by the distended stomachs, thin extremities, and pouchy faces that come from extended use of HIV drugs. Another is a glistening young black man whose body is thick and thin in all the right places. The Korean men utterly ignore me and the three gay men give me a quick assessment before returning to their poses.

The pool itself is an enormous tiled expanse of steaming water that smells gently of sulfur. I lower myself into the wet heat inch by inch, savoring the heavy silkiness of the water, moving slowly because the first immersion is always the most delicious. Finally, I let myself fall backward, under the water, and just float there for a few moments. Half walking, half swimming, I make my way to the fountain at the center of the pool that is the source of the mineral water. I reach up and sweep great armfuls of the thick water onto my head. Finally, I settle onto the ledge at the far side of the fountain where I can relax in privacy.

During those first months of sobriety, when it was raining as it has been lately, I would come to the same spot late in the morning, sit in the water, and cry at how completely I had fucked up my life. Dino was gone. New York was gone. I'd lost or run away from everything I loved and found myself in a strange city where I knew no one. When I felt completely lost, the water helped by washing off the filth of my past. At the very least, immersing myself in the steaming world of the spa would eventually make me so deliriously relaxed that I wanted nothing but to go home and sleep.

Ultimately, the magic of the springs comes not only from the hot water but also from plunging at intervals into an icy menthol pool. The first dip into the ice water, after having given way to the womblike hot pool, is unbearable. The water is so cold that it burns and, as opposed to the hot pool, I plunge into the coldness as quickly as possible, submerging myself entirely until my body starts to become numb and tingle. After a few more moments, a wonderful trancelike state overtakes my mind and I can remain in the freezing water for quite some time. Finally, I stumble out of the coldness and step back into the warmth again, each wave of heat feeling like a thousand pinpricks. After repeating this process four or five times, I can barely think, let alone indulge in my constant state of worry.

Immersed in the water, I know that most of my pain comes from the fact that I want to control everything. If I drop down into the water here, let myself drift and float loose, there are no rapids that I will tumble over. There are no depths in which I will drown. But still I hold onto the edge. Judy told me that I don't know what I want or where I'm headed and that it's fine. I want to believe that.

I fell asleep early this evening after returning from the Hot Springs. I slept without dreaming but have woken up now in the middle of the night. I was shuffling through channels on the television when I came across *Wings of Desire*. I've seen the movie twice but had forgotten about it. The film is mostly in utterly flat German with the exception of scenes with Peter Falk, who strangely appears in the film looking very much like Detective Colombo, the character that brought him fame. First, Dino and I saw it in a theater in New York. The second time I saw it was in Rome, where Dino and I had taken an apartment for the summer. The Italians dispensed with subtitles altogether, dubbing the dialogue into Italian. So ultimately I've never really paid attention to the dialogue of the movie and tonight I only read about half of the subtitles because they are annoyingly cut off on my television screen.

There is something very beautiful about the movie. Set in Berlin and shot in the tones of a fine silver gelatin print, the film is about angels. Everything shimmers dully. The angels look exactly like the living people they quietly observe. Carrying notebooks, the angels carefully record the strange, small, telling moments that somehow define humanity. They are doing more than observing though. The angels are witnesses who sometimes stand behind loved ones, a hand resting on a sobbing shoulder. The living person never knows why, but there is a little wave of comfort that passes over them as the angel smiles sadly.

In the film, only children can see the angels. The children are not afraid of the strange figures standing and watching daily life. Rather, the angel and child smile knowingly at one another. I realize that I've never bothered to think about what the movie means. I just watch it. Tonight, I wish that there were a way to be like a kid again so that I could see the angels who must be sitting around my bed, watching me. Maybe one has his hand on me now because I'm falling back asleep.

Chapter 8

THE LOST ISLAND OF MANHATTAN

I first met Hisako at Area in the '80s during the short period when I lived in New York without Dino. She could usually be found standing in the entry hall in front of the display cases that were changed monthly to reflect a different theme. The first time I saw her she was positioned in front of a display case next to Andy Warhol. They were both wearing masks. Warhol's mask consisted of a face covered with thick pancake makeup, whereas Hisako wore a slightly disturbing wooden monkey mask.

When I walked up and stood next to Hisako, she turned to me, her monkey mask tilting slightly to the side. In a nearly impenetrable Japanese accent she said, "You make picture of Hisako monkey mask in Andy Warhol."

"In Andy Warhol?"

She thrust a camera at me and indicated the shutter release with a bony finger. "Andy Warhol is Hisako picture now."

Her hands shook violently as she handed me the camera. Only years later would I find out that she was shooting heroin. At the time, I simply assumed that she was high on blow like me and everyone else.

I still have a print of that photograph. Hisako's monkey face looks strangely natural on her knotty little body and Warhol looks very much like his usual blank self. I am a shadowy figure briefly reflected in the glass by the glare of the flash. Hisako printed the image as if it had been lit by a bare bulb in someone's basement, all inky blacks with too-white flesh.

Hisako cleaned up and even went to meetings for a while, but she never changed, not even when she found success in the art world. She still lived, I might say squatted, in a loft in New York's meat district, cooking on a hot plate even as the city transformed around her. Almost twenty years after I met her, I received a call from Hisako asking me to write a story to accompany a series of her photographs of New York in the '80s. When she phoned, it was clear that time had not improved her accent. "I make artist book with you me pictures and story that you."

"What?"

"My dealer call tomorrow." And she was gone. The next day her dealer did phone, sounding exhausted by decades of trying to understand Hisako's wishes and translate them to the outside world. It turned out that Hisako had an offer to publish a book of her photographs of the streets of New York. Rather than the usual essay by an important curator or critic interpreting the photographs, she wanted a story that related to them emotionally rather than literally. A CD arrived a few days later containing hundreds of images that Hisako had taken in the '80s. In an act of patience that could only have been inspired by heroin, she had stood in the streets of Manhattan with her huge viewfinder camera and waited until there was not a single person or moving car in sight. Then she would click the shutter. The images were sad and lonely, just the way I remembered New York. They captured perfectly the feeling of being in one of the most crowded cities on earth and feeling utterly alone. I said yes immediately and now, three months later, I have been summoned to New York to help Hisako place the text of my story within a series of her images.

Upon reaching New York, I find a cab immediately outside the United Terminal and slip through light traffic, under the East River, and into Manhattan. The fatigue of the flight melts away as the cab emerges from the tunnel and turns in the direction of a sign that reads, "Downtown." I am absorbed in rhythms and sounds as the driver weaves to narrowly avoid pedestrians who aggressively walk into traffic. Each one, whether a business woman in a sternly tailored suit or a towering, shirtless black man, stakes out territory by standing as perilously close to traffic as possible. Each one stares with bravado and hatred at the driver who dares to impede his or her progress. The cab hopscotches its way over to Lexington, past the Indian restaurants and groceries, and then turns westward on Twenty-third Street. Skirting the upper edge of gay Chelsea and the lower edge of the gentrified art world, we make our way to Ninth Avenue before finally plunging down into the meat district.

Much to Hisako's landlord's consternation, she had kept the same loft for years, doggedly paying the low rent on time and ignoring the sporadic water service in the building. Most tenants had been driven out by the building's decay or had given in to buyout offers. But the landlord had underestimated Hisako. The meat district had become very chic but, when I had first met Hisako in the mid-'80s, it was still a wild outpost on the edge of the Village, containing mostly gay bars, meat markets, and whores. The whores were particularly colorful: gaudy transvestites mixing with real women, all walking unsteadily down the center of cobblestone streets in dirty spike heels. In winter, the trannies would wear long furs and parade up and down Ninth Avenue. When a car or truck approached, they would open their coats like butterfly wings, revealing naked bodies, plastic tits, and tucked cocks in thongs. Some nights Hisako would wordlessly cook us a marvelous Japanese meal on her hot plate. We would put two chairs by the loft's windows and spend the evening eating from our laps, watching the show unfold outside the window.

The streets were always slick with grease, especially in summer, when a hundred years of drippings would liquefy. The thing about the meat district that most fascinated me in those years was the physical space of the neighborhood. In the morning, the streets would be filled with trucks jutting out perpendicular to the warehouses, blocking the street and forcing one to weave in and out. In the late afternoon, the trucks would disappear briefly, leaving the streets entirely unblocked and, with the lowness of the buildings, the neighborhood seemed more open to the sky than anywhere else in Manhattan. In the evening, just past dusk, the trucks would appear again, but parallel parked in double or triple rows, again narrowing the streets and creating a sort of maze. There was just enough room for bodies to slip between the trucks and one would hear an occasional thud or groan when walking past. So the streets would expand and contract like blood vessels, pumping throughout the days and nights, endlessly alive.

I haven't been back to New York in several years and, as the cab pulls up at the corner of Fourteenth and Ninth, I see that the neighborhood has gentrified even further than when I was here last. The meat markets are still here, shuttered behind steel gates, waiting to open at four or five in the morning when the teamsters arrive. But the markets and the cobblestone streets are now set pieces interspersed with sleek restaurants and boutiques. It is too early for the whores, only a little past nine, but it looks as if when they appear, they will make as much money posing for pictures with tourists as turning tricks. I gather my bags and cross the street, fumbling with my cell phone, feeling somehow self-conscious as young, rich, drunk, impossibly glamorous people surge past. The women wear pastel colors on the filthy street and the men tend towards leather jackets and jeans with expensive shoes. They carefully navigate broken wooden pallets and dumpsters filled to overflowing. On loading platforms, hipsters sit smoking and talking on cells. Down the block, a movie shoot is in progress and the ancient, noble building being used as a backdrop looks trapped and sheepish flooded with the harsh lights.

The meat district has been converted into a parody of its former self, to be enjoyed by those who would not have appreciated what went on there before. They want the appearance of sex and danger but not the reality of it splashing up on a silk dress or an alligator boot. Much money has been spent making the meat district appear as if it is still rough, but everywhere are hints of luxury like brushed aluminum window frames and designer doors.

Hisako's door is still unmarked by any number and stubbornly unequipped with a buzzer so I call her on my cell. When she answers, it is not with a hello but with a half shout, "I come!"

In a moment, Hisako flies down the stairs and pulls the door open. As always, I try to hug her but she allows herself only to be pressed against me for a fraction of a second before pulling away. "Come," she says, glancing over her shoulder and out the door to the noisy street. "This shit," she mumbles and grabs my bag.

We begin to mount a rickety staircase leading up to lofts that, with the exception of Hisako's, probably now rent for thousands of dollars a month. The stairwell is foul, replete with a glassine envelope and a syringe lying on the first step where someone sat to do what they had to do. There is the distinct, sharp smell of cat piss. The walls are a flaking composite of metal and insulation. With each step, the stairs moan with deep resignation. On the second floor landing, the water heaters sit, exposed, buzzing ominously in a row. Electrical boxes jut from the wall with wire tentacles reaching in all directions, and a hammer lies on the floor from some repair effort abandoned midway. Hisako turns a key in the lock of the industrial security door that separates the stairwell from the interior hallway and slips inside.

A large photograph hangs in the hallway, next to her door. It has always been here and I'd often asked Hisako about it but she'd always just smiled and ignored me. The picture is a grisly image of a man sitting in a chair with a shotgun between his legs. His head is entirely blown away, missing. A crime scene photographer must have taken it but someone else had blown it up to epic proportions, giving it a certain mythic tone. The body sits in a recliner in a typical suburban living room, dressed in a neat white button-down shirt and tan slacks. The victim had carefully taken off his shoes and put them next to the chair as if to relax for the evening: a normal man on a normal night who'd put a shotgun in his mouth.

Hisako opens her front door, slips off her flip-flops, and reminds me with a glance that I am expected to do the same. Having laces, it takes me a moment, teetering against the wall to extract my feet, still swollen from the flight, from my leather shoes. I wonder how the loft has changed and, as I enter, the answer is immediately apparent: not at all. The door closes behind me and Hisako's hand darts out to lock it securely, slipping the chain into place. In the gathering darkness of early evening, reflected car lights race across the ceiling of the huge space. Small patches of color from neon signs illuminate the walls. I walk across the expanse of the living and dining room to the tall windows. Hisako follows me and unlocks a window. She pushes it up and the din of the city rolls into the room like a thick fog. Drunken screams, laughter, car horns, and blasts of salsa merge into the howling roar of the city. Hisako retreats to turn on the lights and I admire the loft. Where the street and stairs had been filthy, the loft is sleek and white. The floor, walls, ceiling, and furnishings are all perfectly white. Hisako had always tirelessly scrubbed every scuffmark from the floor. The desolate purity of the place is further enhanced by the monochromatic art on the walls. A large Marden drawing, a Twombly, and a LeWitt are the stars, reflecting Hisako's growing success and attendant bank account. One entire wall is filled with drawings made by a young artist with clear water on paper, the sheets of white just slightly stained by the brush strokes. While the loft could have been cold and dead, it is redeemed by the counterpoint of the decaying building and enlivened by the cacophony of the street.

After presenting me with a glass of cool green tea, Hisako murmurs, "You unpack now." The wave of her hand indicates that I will be sleeping on the low sofa near the window. But I just sit in the living room, not unpacking. I listen to the city and try to pick out individual voices from snatches of conversation. My body tingles with the rush of being here again, the Los Angeles languor draining from me, replaced by the forward motion of New York. Looking out the windows, my eyes are drawn to the dirty building across the street. It has escaped all renovation efforts and sits as the sole reminder of what the neighborhood once was. Referred to as the Triangle Building, it was built on the island formed by the convergence of Ninth Avenue and Hudson. Its reddish pink bricks are stained by years of filth, some of the windows boarded over, rusting steel fire escapes puncturing the uneven skin with innumerable signs that had been painted on and then scrubbed off. Haphazard electrical and cable wires hang between windows, surely only a few of them legally installed. Someone had begun an urban garden on one of the fire escapes and then abandoned it; the expired plants were punctuated by the occasional bloom of a rose bush that refused to die. The upper four floors of the building house many artists and others that had been or hoped still to become artists. The windows of the second floor have been mysteriously covered with orange paper backed by dim lights, giving the effect of an evil, glowing jack-o'-lantern.

On the ground level, a black steel staircase plunges down below the street next to a sign reading, "Manhole." This was formerly the Hellfire Club, which provided a reasonable facsimile of Hades as decorated by a serial killer. Although it has been renamed, I refuse to think of it as anything other than the Hellfire. I had been there many times even though it was straight on alternate nights, and remember clearly how the cold stone walls became slick with sweat as an evening progressed. Tattered sofas sat close by metal cages. The club, which seemed small at first, was maze-like with a number of interesting hidden nooks and doors that opened into strange, small rooms. In fact the architecture of the club was fluid, a previously open room might be unexplainably closed one weekend but another previously hidden nook opened to reveal a new sexual setting. The space seemed alive. The club was famously the favorite hangout of Andrew Crispo, a New York art dealer accused of being involved in the S/M murder of a male model where the victim's body was found wearing a leather bondage mask. For years after the murder, the tabloid press had been filled with stories of the Hellfire's Mafia connections, coke-fueled S/M, and snuff films.

I feel ignited. New York is a drug, shooting jolts of electricity into me, demanding that I be a part of it again. I walk slowly around the loft a few times before going back to the window. A tall blond woman strides briskly along the street and I can hear her stiletto heels on the sidewalk. She wears black leather pants, a tight white T-shirt and a long black trench coat that billows behind her as she glides down the steps past the doorman standing at the entrance to the Hellfire. He seems almost to bow to her. Something builds in me and my groin aches. Every inch of me wants to throw myself into this city and let it take me. How stupid I had been to think that the sunshine of California could erase all of this.

Hisako is back now. Her patience is limited and she thrusts a roughly bound book at me. "You look now and I was work."

"What?"

"Tonight . . . work."

"I thought I'd go for a walk, maybe we'd have dinner."

"You walk. I work." She places the book in my hands now. "First, you make sure story good. All put in."

I just nod my head, not really wanting to do this now but knowing it is easier than watching her pace around the loft, waiting. Both the book and my story are titled, *Happiness*. As I flip through it, I see that Hisako has broken my short story into a paragraph, sometimes only a line per page and linked the text to her lonely photos. I stop at a few of them. The Cathedral of St. John the Divine sits behind a huge pile of black earth, as if attending its own burial. Fourteenth Street, which hums just below me, is entirely empty in another photo, looking atypically fresh and open to the sky and river.

"It looks great, Hisako."

She doesn't stamp her foot but she approximates it with a little shake of her head, her blunt cut black hair switching. "No, you read. After this, too late. Mistakes no."

"Oh, OK. You mean you want me to proof it?"

"Proof," she says with another swing of her hair as she turns on a lamp next to the sofa for emphasis and leaves the room.

I'm not quite sure why it was necessary to fly across the

country to proof the book in person but, after all, I'd wanted an excuse to get away from L.A. anyway. So I settle in and carefully begin to turn the pages, watching my story spread out leisurely alongside the sad images. The text is an odd little tale of a boy who walks through an empty city looking for someone to play with. He wanders around calling out, "Hello," but never hears an answer. His mother tells him never to go into the Carnival but, one day, he cannot resist when he calls out and a voice answers him, saying, "Hello, there." In the Carnival's Hall of Mirrors, he sees his reflection and smashes it, destroying himself. Hisako had thought the story was hopeful when she first read it and told me, "Like me the drinking. Kill myself to start over." She was right.

As soon as I give Hisako my approval for the text, she disappears into her studio without a word, closing the door softly but firmly behind her. Dismissed, I walk out of the loft, drawn by the thunder of New York, with no clear destination in mind, simply setting out to walk in the night. Opening the sheet of paper I'd printed out at home with the local C.M.A. meetings, I discover that a meeting is scheduled to begin nearby in twenty minutes. I'm full of resentment that crystal has come to New York. It seemed like the one thing that Los Angeles had before New York, although I know it's hardly something to be proud of. I've already constructed a narrative of how the meetings will be different in New York than in Los Angeles—ruined, pretentious, and political. Even now as I make the decision not to go to a meeting, I can feel that it is a mistake. I tell myself that I'll go tomorrow.

I will always carry a map of Manhattan in my head. Here and there I've marked Manhattan with my scent, like a dog marking its territory. My Manhattan begins here in the meat district, extends upward only to Times Square, pushes slightly into the East Village and ends in TriBeCa. This circumscribed Manhattan was "Downtown" in the early '80s. Though Times Square is not usually associated with "Downtown," I'd always given it honorary status because at the time, it was still bleak and scary and wonderful.

For me, New York has always been about walking. And my best walks take place at night. Sometimes the walks have a destination but many times they simply reflect my desire to be immersed in the possibilities of the night. Tonight I decide to completely ignore the meat district until my return because I know it will then be late when I return and the place will have a better chance of being as I remember it. Instead, I head east on Fourteenth Street towards Eighth Avenue, the main thoroughfare of gay Chelsea. What were once abandoned buildings or decrepit squats are now hair salons and stores with polished concrete floors that seem to sell nothing but a few perfectly placed belts, coiled like rattlesnakes, daring someone to grab them.

It was on this block that I met, for the first, last and only time, the late great Leigh Bowery. He had been staying with the clothing designer Stephen Sprouse and, through some confluence of drugs and timing, I'd been invited to an apartment where the great Ms. Bowery was preparing for a night out. These were the days before Lucien Freud had painted Bowery's drapes of white flesh in London. In London, Bowery ruled the nightworld but in New York he was known only by an inner circle that admired his devotion to the unwearable costumes he would create and model when he came to town.

I had a mad crush on Sprouse, who was a second-generation punk, known for spray-painting his name on expensive jackets and dresses of his own design. With his stalks of black hair extending over his white face and kohl-rimmed eyes, I thought he was beyond sexy. But I was with Dino and Sprouse was with heroin so the best I ever got was an occasional opportunity to hang with him. Bowery was part of Sprouse's orbit and on that night he was getting ready as Stephen and I lay on the bed watching TV. Leigh would twirl into the room every half hour or so with another iteration of her costume, presenting it for Stephen's approval. Depending on how high he was, Stephen would either adjust it, rip it a bit, or just nod his approval before closing his eyes.

I still recall the outfit Bowery settled upon well after midnight. It was something like an enormous, sequined caftan that covered not only his entire six-foot-plus frame but also his head. It was a hideously compelling green and black pattern and there were cutouts for his eyes, adorned with enormous false eyelashes, and his mouth. Through holes in his cheeks, Leigh had used safety pins to attach giant red plastic lips in front of his real lips. The caftan, corseted to push his folds of fatty flesh into the shape of breasts, flared out from an empire waist. Underneath, Bowery wore matching tights and a pair of acid green heels.

I can't remember where we went that night when Leigh was finally ready. I had the feeling that the getting ready was more important than the going out in any case. The last thing I remember was Bowery, looking like he was eight feet tall, teetering down the street toward a cab on Eighth Avenue. He was as polite as a great English lady, waving to the Puerto Rican kids who screamed in disbelief when they saw him, nodding his head to the leather queens passing by, and even blowing kisses to the trannie prostitutes. To each one, he would warble, "Good evening! Hello!" I never saw Stephen or Leigh Bowery again. They are now both dead; Stephen's heart failed and Bowery was lost to AIDS.

The streets of New York are thick with ghosts who seem more real than the clean-cut boys rushing down Eighth Avenue towards me. Gone are the leather-clad men and the shady hustlers. New York and L.A. were once charged elements, opposites, sparking between the coasts. But the distance between these opposing cities has collapsed. They've folded together like advertisements facing one another in a glossy magazine, creating something smeared with media ink. Here is the local Starbucks where the boys meet. Across the avenue is the Restoration Hardware where they buy stuff to decorate their apartments.

I practically run up Eighth Avenue, past shiny new restaurants that were once stinking bars. I feel like an old man, nostalgic for a youth that never really existed. Chelsea used to end at Twenty-third Street, blurring into a mix of industrial buildings filled with commercial printers, then giving way to the grimy rush of Penn Station and Port Authority, and finally disappearing into the secretive humming of the rag trade. Now, the suburbia of Chelsea has pushed itself up the avenue and many of my landmarks have been lost to make way for new condos.

Gone is the apartment building where I had a regular Monday night trick while Dino thought I was at an ACT UP meeting. His name was Sal or Tony or Paul and he was a perfect example of a sweet Italian guy who worked for some obscure city agency that paid him just enough for a tiny apartment in the proximity of unlimited sex. His thing was poppers. He lived on the little brown bottles containing a toxic brew that did God knows what to our brains. Our primary sex act could have been called *frottage* had it been more focused. Tony's thing was to make out and squirm around in bed, covered in oil, which was not such a bad thing considering that he looked like a marble statue. Tony's apartment smelled of the cheap oil he used to smear all over us (and which I could not possibly have gotten rid of during the quick shower that followed our sessions). So every Monday night I would emerge from his tawdry apartment, reeking of oil and poppers, with a pounding headache. I remember always running into a Korean deli on my way home to buy a carton of chocolate milk that, for some reason, seemed to quiet my throbbing brain.

With the advent of cell phones, there are almost no pay phones left in New York. When I see one, I stop even though I have my cell in my pocket. This is something I do every time I am in New York. I stop and call from a pay phone because it will not show my name on a caller ID. I call my friend Lee to see if he's still alive.

Dino and I had been living in New York for several years when I met my best friend Lee on Easter Sunday 1988, surrounded by drunken Brits. Each Easter in New York, a shifting group of British expats and their friends walk in the New York Easter Parade. The group is loosely defined, drawn together by fashion sense, loneliness for the homeland, sexuality, snobbishness and, most of all, a disdain for their adopted home, the United States of America. It takes a certain type of self-loathing, as an American, to be part of such a group and I was perfectly suited to membership.

I was seduced, literally, into their midst by an Englishman who was the most charming man I'd ever met. When I first moved to New York and was a desperately unhappy waiter in an Upper East Side café, Peter began to show up each afternoon to hold court, sip coffee, and romance me relentlessly. Perhaps because Dino had run off to Italy with his sculptor or because I was twenty-one years old, I was desperate to be swept away by someone sophisticated and exotic. Peter, with his down market English accent, pirate earrings, and heavy goatee, was exactly that. He was the first man to tell me I was beautiful. His attention and insistence on having me was intoxicating.

There was a downside to Peter, though. He was a drunk. The exact traits that so charmed me—his humor, street sense, and lasciviousness—would turn ugly when he drank. Because my liver was drying out from Hepatitis B, I wasn't drinking and barely doing drugs at the time so Peter's stumbling and groping were less appealing than they might have been either earlier or later in my life. I never minded so much that he would fuck anything in pants. I hated that he would also tell them that they were beautiful.

When, a few months into our courtship, he presented me with a Concorde ticket to join him in London, I lost my senses and gave way. Never having been to Europe, I was unprepared for the wave of jet lag that washed over me even with the benefit of supersonic transport. I spent the majority of the trip either sleeping or thinking about Dino while Peter became increasingly frustrated. When I returned to New York, I learned that Dino's mother had died and I began to lure him to New York for weekends, gradually coercing him into moving from Pittsburgh to live with me. Peter, ever the charmer, decided the way to save face was to include both of us in his social life. "No problem, mate," he'd say.

Peter loved to organize and the Easter Parade was his favorite event. Each year had a theme and we would all work on our costumes for months in advance. Though they were snobbish, the English respected the power of the press and, invariably, Bill Cunningham from the *Times* would appear on Fifth Avenue to snap our get-ups as we wove through the pedestrian throngs of old ladies in tulle hats and dogs dressed in bonnets. The year I met Lee, Peter had decreed the theme to be "Pearly Kings and Queens." I had absolutely no idea what a Pearly King was and, when I asked Peter, he imperiously told me to "look it up." I learned that the "Pearlies" were Victorian street vendors and, after a big shipment of pearl buttons from Japan, they had taken to encrusting their clothes with pearl buttons, sewing them into great swirls and designs that were both vulgar and chic in the way the English so love. Aside from being a kind of advertisement, the pearl designs all signified different messages, from a horseshoe meaning luck to playing cards symbolizing that life is a gamble.

Never one comfortable in costumes, I sewed a few pearl buttons on the seams of a vest and wore it that day. (Dino, scornful of the whole thing, dressed head to toe in unadorned but irreproachable Sulka and called it a day.) We all gathered at Peter's apartment on Central Park South to get dead drunk before the parade. Peter barely gave my vest a look before sniffing, "Bit twee, isn't it, mate?" He swirled his vodka and orange derisively and turned to greet other guests whose chic black clothes glittered with ornate sprays of sparkling pearl buttons.

I noticed a tall man with a particularly outrageous long black jacket over skin-tight trousers. His coat was adorned with a giant design of a flowerpot sprouting blooms of playing cards, anchors, crosses, hearts, and doves. His dyed black hair hung well below his shoulders and he swept it back as he hoisted a canapé into his mouth. Looking at me, he licked his newly empty fingers and smiled before settling onto a sofa with me.

"That's an amazing jacket," I told Lee. "I'm Patrick."

"Thanks. Lee," he responded in a honky New Jersey accent, bussing my cheek.

"It must have taken you days to sew it."

Lee, as he would countless times in the future, drew his long hair in front of both of our faces for privacy and whispered, "Glue gun, girl. Now how about we head to the potty and do some blow?"

Lee's age was always a well-kept secret but I suspect he

was at least ten years older than I. He was a tall Jewish queen from New Jersey who had inherited his mother's sharp tongue. Lee's mother liked diet pills and affectionately referred to her husband as "you fat fuck."

Lee had the aura of a Warhol Superstar: damaged but resilient, eccentric to the point of aggravation. Lee was my constant companion for the next ten years and we spent much of that time in the potty snorting coke and crystal, gobbling X, and tripping on blotter acid. Being asthmatic, Lee didn't care for pot but he never met a vodka martini he didn't like and was, in fact, a much better drunk than a junkie. When the word "cocktail" bounced from Lee's lips, it conjured visions of long nights and thrilling adventures. Lee often drew a martini glass next to his signature, a part of his name. In fact, he drew them everywhere, always tilted slightly to the side as if they were in the process of being emptied. Lee and I drank extra dry Absolut martinis with three olives. For a while, I adored everything about him.

The two of us soon had a list of our favorite spots. He'd call and say, "Meet me at our coffee shop." Without asking, I'd know that he meant the Cozy Soup-N-Burger on Broadway. Or I'd leave a message saying, "Meet me at our bar." Our bar was a seedy Puerto Rican hustler bar called Trix on Forty-eighth Street between Broadway and Eighth Avenue. From the first time the doorman at Trix frisked us for guns, we knew we'd found our spot. The house drink was a poisonous concoction called a Star Trek that was a vodka grapefruit with a swirl of viscous orange liqueur. Many of the working boys came not only to turn tricks but because the owner of the bar would set out an enormous pot of macaroni and cheese. After a few Star Treks and whatever drug we favored that week, we would slip into the booth at the back of the bar where the

same two tragic drag queens often sat eating take-out slices of pizza. Lee often combed out their wigs in the bathroom or reapplied their mascara, telling them that they were "fierce."

Lee loved props and always carried a bag that, like a magician's hat, produced unexpected objects. We were sitting with the drag queens at the back table in Trix one night when he extracted a bottle of eye drops, applied them until his eyes were overflowing and turning to them, wailing, "Oh, you poor girls. You pooooor, poooor girls." Despite, indeed, because of the fact this made no sense, he repeated the phrase, reapplying drops, until the drag queens were shrieking with laughter. Lee seemed to me to have been created for the sole purpose of delighting me.

Not just a silly queen, Lee delighted in every sexual perversion. Another night at Trix, he drew me to a side table and told me that he had a new trick who was into scat. I pretended to be naïve, "Scat? What's that?"

"Oh, child," Lee murmured, "you know . . . poop."

I made the mistake of refusing to believe this so Lee ordered us another round of Star Treks. When he had drained half the glass, he hauled his bag onto the table and extracted a small Tupperwear containing a turd. He continued to root around in his bag, mumbling, "Damn, I forgot the spoon."

Lee and I both had plenty of tricks, even though we both had boyfriends. His boyfriend was an alcoholic, even more advanced in his disease than Lee, who had often passed out by early evening. Lee and I were each other's alibis. If I didn't make it home until four in the morning, it was because I'd been dancing with Lee. We were, in fact, often together until morning but neither of us had been dancing. Instead, we picked nightspots where we could both socialize and fuck.

We particularly liked the sex clubs of the East Village, with their seemingly endless warrens of little booths, where we could each set up shop in a stall. Every hour or so, we would take a break, share whatever drugs we had (we both always kept a stash we wouldn't admit to until the other begged for it) and catch up on the night's progress so far.

We all have that one friend, to call them an enabler is too easy, who delights in the behaviors that horrify everyone else in our lives. Lee was the friend who found my blackouts charming, who applauded my eccentric taste in sexual partners, and who proudly regaled everyone with tales of my exploits. He was my witness. Lee was there to see me throw a drink in the face of another drunk, there to help me seduce a businessman from Philly with a pocketful of coke, there to cheer me on as I rampaged through my life.

I have a short attention span whereas Lee was obsessively interested in people, especially when they could provide drugs or alcohol. I preferred just buying my own and minimizing contact with others. But Lee would stop by a certain bar every afternoon to chat with the same burned-out old waitress and work her for free drinks. He would cook Thanksgiving dinner for our drug dealer along with his brother, wife, and child. While he certainly enjoyed the free drugs and drinks, Lee had the talent of being interested in anyone marginal or extreme, including me.

Lee loved to accompany me on business trips. The destination didn't have to be glamorous as long as it involved a free hotel and meals. There was something about hotels that was fascinating to Lee and the idea that someone else was paying for it made the whole experience transcendent for him. I was once forced to give a lecture in Buffalo and Lee happily signed on for the interminable drive after I promised him that we would stay in Buffalo's best hotel. The first few hours of the drive flew past due to a gram of coke, which was the entirety of my drug stash for the trip. Because we had stopped at McDonald's on the way out of the city, we were snorting the coke through enormous Happy Meal straws that devoured the lines. I knew Lee was holding but he wouldn't come clean until we were already in Buffalo, crashing, and exceedingly cranky.

When we got to Buffalo, we were both coming down and on edge even before we discovered that Buffalo's finest hotel was little more than a glorified Motel 6. Still, it offered room service and, as he settled in to unpack his toiletries, Lee ordered martinis and shrimp cocktail via room service. It was already evening and, once the rubbery shrimp and drinks had been consumed, Lee revealed that he had not only more coke but also hits of X for both of us.

Within hours, Lee and I were gloriously high and rubbing elbows with the locals at a gay bar. The bar's claim to fame was that it had been firebombed the week before but the X gave it a sparkle. Soon enough, Lee headed off to a bathhouse and I had hooked up with a gentleman of a certain age who lived in a basement. The next thing I knew the gray morning light of Buffalo was leaking down the staircase of that very same basement. I was horrified when the morning light revealed with whom I had spent the night. However, I had little time for reflection when I realized that I had a total of one hour to return to the hotel, shower, and get to my lecture at the university.

When I returned to the hotel, Lee had already showered and was sitting with an enormous pot of room service coffee and assorted pastries, his wet hair wrapped in a turban. He stared at me and gasped, "What the fuck happened to your eye?"

It seemed that during the previous night's encounter I had somehow gotten what could only have been semen into my right eye, which had turned bright red. Lee produced his ever-present bottle of Visine but it had absolutely no effect. We were soon out the door, in the car, and on the way to my lecture but, as we pulled into the parking lot, the car ran out of gas. As I was already considerably late, the professor who had invited me to speak was waiting at the front door of his building and watched in amazement as Lee, in his high-heeled Spanish boots, pushed our car into the parking lot with me steering and screaming at him to hurry.

These experiences did not shock Lee because he had been an addict for so long. He had also been doing speed, in its many guises, since art school. His breakfast in school was iced coffee and a few Black Beauties. Lee was too old to have been on Ritalin as a child but, later, he and his mother got twin Dexedrine prescriptions for weight loss. He always loved taking "dolls" and would sometimes produce a Bennie from his bag, admire it for a moment, and gulp it down without comment.

I'd done my share of Black Beauties, Robin's Eggs and Bennies in college but my thing was coke. The first time Lee and I did crystal it didn't have a name in New York and, indeed, we didn't even know we were buying it. I knew as soon as I opened the envelope that it was something different. It had a sickening, yellow cast to it and a faint chemical odor. I just thought it was bad coke but I didn't complain because it was cheap and powerful. When I told Lee I thought the coke was cut with speed, he nodded and said, "Fabulous."

One day, Lee and I were walking down Second Avenue on our way to the Nightingale Bar where our drug dealer could be found every afternoon. Lee was wearing enormous wraparound sunglasses in the February gloom, his hair pulled into a tight bun. I was wearing my usual ratty leather jacket with a disheveled pair of black velvet pants and Frye boots. I remember that particular day clearly because I turned to him as we walked through the East Village and said, "We're addicts, right?" Without a word, Lee stopped in the street, pulled his sunglasses down just far enough so that he could wink at me, and took my hand. We kept on walking.

Lee changed that very day and maybe I did too but I couldn't see it. What had been sweet and outrageous in Lee when he was primarily drinking became nasty and bitter as our drug use grew. Our lies to each other increased. When we would make one of our occasional pledges to one another to stop using, we would later find that we had both been busily snorting our way through the period of supposed sobriety. As my drive for drug-fueled sexual abandon increased, I grew resentful of the hours spent trying to organize Lee into leaving his apartment. And, on his end, he was hurt by my nightly rush to ditch him for uninterrupted sex.

There were certain situations that were so hideous that only Lee could transform them. Dino once had a seizure and collapsed in the perfume department of Bergdorf Goodman's. Sobbing on the phone to Lee, I was taken aback when he whispered, "A seizure at Bergdorf's? That's the most glamorous thing I've ever heard! Just hold on, baby. I'll meet you at St. Vincent's."

When Lee arrived in the Emergency Room that day, I was already in a screaming fight with two young black girls. These two had watched as Dino was wheeled in and gave me the once over as I sat down to wait. I was wearing a pair of Dino's Wallabees that day and they immediately began to whisper. Understandably, I was in no mood and glared at them, "You got a problem with me?"

One of the girls had the audacity to stand up, cross the room and point at my shoes with her long fingernail. She cocked her head and said, "Shit! Those shoes be stupid!"

I had just given the girl a nice shove when Lee arrived and flung himself between us. Within ten minutes one of the girls was holding my hand as I cried while Lee was touching up the polish on the other's nails. An hour later, after Dino had been taken upstairs to a room, Lee was kissing the girls and making arrangements to meet them for drinks later.

Then Dino died and Lee again proved himself to be absolutely loyal to me in my moment of need. When I told Lee that I wanted to steal Dino's credit cards after his death, Lee did not chastise me but went along and got a laptop himself. When I cried and raged during blackouts, Lee probably just held me and then mixed me another drink. Lee never judged me and, with his acceptance, set a standard that I could never live up to.

Lee was chronically underemployed and drifted from selling furniture in a SoHo showroom to hawking industrial carpet. Every week brought a different career plan. He was an extraordinary illustrator though, and produced an entire line of queeny but brilliant greeting cards, which were never sold; they joined his canvases from art school in a storage locker. His shocking interior designs (including the one for his own tiny apartment that featured orange tile in the exact hue used by McDonald's) were never realized in clients' homes. His amazing capacity for comedy never yielded a career as a writer or performer.

The job he loved, and was perhaps most suited to, was as a phone sex operator. Having been discharged from another sales job, Lee saw an ad for a phone sex line that he had already thoroughly enjoyed calling on a regular basis. There was no denying that Lee was qualified—he loved sex and talking on the phone. He was the kind of friend who would stay on the phone with you to watch TV from different locations, only occasionally discussing the program. He was quite happy to stay on the phone with me until we had both fallen asleep. I would be dimly aware, a few hours later, that Lee had resumed the conversation whether or not I was awake. Lee became part of my subconscious.

The start of Lee's phone sex job corresponded with his newfound interest in coke and crystal. Because everything became sexual to us when we were high, Lee would happily work double shifts on the lines, taking breaks only to snort and then return to the nasty talk. Lee could work all the lines—from Chicks With Dicks to the Cellblock—and had a different persona for each. He created his favorite character, named Ashanga, for the Chicks With Dicks line. He would describe himself as a six foot black "woman" with cornrows, killer titties and a fat uncut cock.

After Lee secured the caller's credit card, the clock would start to tick. As I well knew, time seemed to disappear when talking to Lee and many callers were probably shocked to find that they had reached orgasm in the first five minutes of the call but remained on the line for another hour chatting with their fantasy "girl."

The manager of the phone sex lines was a semi-hot, seemingly straight Puerto Rican guy, José, upon whom Lee focused his full sexual energy. I was more than a little jealous when Lee began to devote his free hours to José but I knew he was like a pit bull with a hot dog and trying to get the treat away from him could prove dangerous. Armed with plenty of drugs and the boredom of the windowless office, Lee would probably have succeeded in his quest to bed José had he not received a call from an elderly man named Stan in Queens.

Lee never told me what Stan's particular kink was but it seemed that his greatest pleasure was simply to speak to Lee for hours on end. Stan was homebound in Queens, due to advanced Parkinson's disease, and utterly alone except for a visiting nurse, paid out of the substantial inheritance Stan had received when his last relative died. The pennies that became a few dollars and eventually hundreds on the phone sex lines mattered little to Stan, who had found a companion in Lee. Finally, a gay man existed who was fascinated in everything about Stan's life. Apparently, Stan was enormously tall, wearing size sixteen shoes, and Lee made it his mission to look in every shoe store on the way home from work each day, inquiring about plus sizes.

Lee shared his problems with Stan, although he never told the old man that he had an alcoholic boyfriend at home. The problem Lee shared with Stan, at length, was his entanglement with the Internal Revenue Service. Lee's efforts at solvency were complicated by the fact that he owed more than twenty thousand dollars to the Internal Revenue Service, which would periodically garnishee his wages. Even Lee's formidable gifts of persuasion proved ineffective with the stern IRS. agent he would occasionally meet with. From the first time Lee mentioned this situation to Stan, the old man offered to pay Lee's debt. Suddenly, the hairy horny Puerto Rican in the front office of the phone sex company disappeared from Lee's mind. He could see, in crystalline detail, the answer to what seemed his ultimate problem.

It was only a matter of time until Lee met Stan. The process began when he asked Stan for his home phone number and called him outside of work. And it was a measure of the situation's importance to Lee that he didn't tell me of his first visit to Stan's house until weeks after it occurred. One night, very late and very drunk, Lee began to fish around in his enormous bag. I had become, or so I thought, immune to being shocked by the bag's contents. However, when Lee produced a carefully folded check from the depths of the bag, it was unlike any of his past displays. He did not flourish it but handed it to me delicately, reverently, and even, I thought, with a hint of shame. This was clearly an important object although it was carried around to every filthy bar and bathhouse in the city. I only later realized that Lee feared his boyfriend might find the check if it were left at home.

Unfolding the check, I registered that it was from Stan's account. That did not surprise me as Lee often borrowed money. However, the amount was unbelievable. The check was made out to Lee for the amount of $24,000 in a shaky hand but signed with firm conviction. Stan's signature was like buying a car that is too expensive, legs shaking as you get in for the first time after completing the paperwork, but stepping on the gas as hard as you can when pulling out of the dealership. I could smell the rubber of tires burning in that signature. Lee had scored.

Lee's disclosure that night was not a confession. He had a serious problem on his hands in that he wasn't sure if the check was good. Lee knew that, as soon as the deposit appeared in his bank account, alarms would go off in the IRS computers, hungrily waiting for payment. As the check was drawn on a Citibank account and I had recently deposited a healthy amount of Dino's money into my account there, I felt confident in taking the check in to determine if it was good. It was indeed. But now Lee had another problem—he didn't want to give the IRS the money. Or at least not all of it. Or maybe none of it.

Having completely torched my own life, I was glad to see someone making even more of a mess of theirs. With all the superiority that comes so naturally to me, I wagged my finger at Lee relentlessly, insisting that he use the windfall to finally resolve his tax problems and be free. After months, he told me that he had paid the IRS but I still have my doubts. However, the genie was out of the bottle with Stan and his bank account. Lee quit his job, which was rapidly falling apart anyway due to his declining relationship with the Puerto Rican manager. Lee's new job was to take care of Stan and, with his laser focus, Lee reorganized his life around the trips to and from a dingy house in Queens. Lee's alcoholic boyfriend was finally jettisoned from the apartment and a major renovation of the tiny space ensued. Computers were purchased to revive Lee's design career. A car was obtained to transport Lee between Manhattan and Queens. Lee bought one of the first tiny cellphones in order to be in constant communication with Stan.

Finally, after so many years of scraping by, Lee was living the life he had fantasized about. True, it involved an ancient and very ill man being allowed to give him blowjobs but Lee didn't let that "harsh his mellow," as he said. The new luxuries even softened the blow of my moving to Los Angeles for no particular reason other than wanting to restart my life.

When I finally got sober, Lee announced on one of my trips back to New York that he had given up drugs and wanted to go to an A.A. meeting with me. I was so happy during the meeting that I kept dissolving into tears. We practically skipped on our way to a celebratory dinner afterward. When I told Lee again how happy I was that he had decided to get sober, he said he was too. Then Lee grasped my hand and ordered a martini. I ordered a Diet Coke and dug deeper into my judgments.

In his new life, Lee had even hired a trainer, managing to shed the extra twenty or thirty pounds he'd always hidden underneath "corrective over-blousing." He looked great, if not quite himself. A few months later, as I was getting into a car to go to the airport for a flight back to Los Angeles, he called to say that he had PCP pneumonia. He had twelve T-cells. And this was from a man who had always used a condom even for blowjobs. Or so he said.

When he told me he was sick, Lee's voice was full of bitterness. "I was so careful and you . . ."

He didn't need to finish because I knew how accurate his statement was. For years, I'd had unsafe sex with Dino before we knew he was infected. Time after time, he shot a bullet inside of me and God moved me aside to safety. It must have seemed to Lee like just another indication of how unfair life could be. Even though we'd been to the same places, done many of the same things, Lee had not escaped whereas I flew free into a new life.

The end of Lee's story is neither dramatic nor inspiring. As he grew sicker, I grew sober in California. As his health waned, mine blossomed again. Everything seemed so fresh and new to me in L.A. that the thought of Lee, sick in the dank streets of Manhattan, was unbearable. After years of watching Dino die, I couldn't watch Lee. So I gradually inched him out of my life with fewer phone calls, a busier schedule, and waves of judgment that were never spoken but always felt between former best friends.

Lee no longer returns my calls, which I no longer make. He gets a Christmas card from me now and remains the last entry on my list of amends still to be made. I know I've joined the list of people whose names on the caller ID cause him to turn away with a shrug and a turned lip. So I only call him from payphones in New York now. When I hear his voice on the answering machine, I don't know if he's OK, but I know he's alive.

I hang up the phone with the sound of Lee's recorded voice still in my ears. I nearly take out my cell phone, thinking that I'll call and leave another message. But then I wonder what the message would be. There is one truth—that I miss Lee and want him to be here now, taking my hand surely in the rush of traffic and leading me to some dive that only he would know about. But the deeper truth is that I don't want our friendship anymore because Lee reminds me of memories that are already too powerful. Even without him as a reminder, those memories and feelings have been crowding into my mind again. Those long nights with him have begun to seem exciting again rather than dangerous. Lee may have moved on to matters such as trying to stay alive but, for me, he remains the person who could go with me no matter how far down I went. I can't have him back. So I run my fingers over the cell phone, then let it drop back down in my pocket as I walk toward Times Square.

On these side streets of the garment district, there were once strange dirty bookstores up flights of stairs. In this industrial building, behind an unmarked door, was a sex club that spread out over an entire floor and opened at four in the morning. Here is the entrance to L'Esqualita, the Latin drag club, where I would wear khakis and make out with homeboys. All of these places remain firmly etched on the map in my head that marks all my nighttime adventures.

Trix is gone, along with the porn theaters and the hustlers. I stand on the corner of Forty-second and Eighth, staring at a blaze of neon signs advertising everything from a fast food restaurant called Chevy's to *The Lion King*. Suddenly, I feel like my whole past has been erased and a wave of anger washes over me. My world has disappeared. I somehow thought that there would be clues to my present discomfort in the past but, instead, New York just makes everything seem more sad and empty. Wherever I'm headed, it's not here.

I take the R train to Astor Place. As I reach the street where the Saint once stood, I know that I never want to come here again. I'm done with this city right now, after only a few hours. I remember sitting one late fall afternoon in a friend's loft in the East Village and looking out his window as a wreck-

ing ball slammed into the side of the Saint, remorselessly ex-
cising it from New York life, making way for another beige
apartment building.

I walk down the street, knowing what I will find, but having to look at it anyway. And here it is. A cheap brass plaque
has been attached to the bland exterior of the Hudson East
apartment building that perches upon the Saint's former site.
It reads:

> *On this site once stood the Loew's Commodore Movie
> Palace, the Fillmore East Theater, and the Saint discothèque.
> Dedicated in celebration of all those who came to watch,
> rock, and dance.*

If Lee taught me anything, it was never to hold back. He
never hesitated to toss a drink in some rude queen's face or
let out a blood-curdling scream when frustrated. I think about
Lee as I look at this cheesy, pathetic plaque that is all that remains of the Saint. What would Lee do?

I read the plaque one more time. *Dedicated in celebration of
all those who came to watch, rock, and dance.* I unzip my pants and
take a good, long piss on it.

I know now I'm through with this place. I'm going home
tomorrow.

Chapter 9

CUFFS

Since I've been back from New York, I'm neither here nor there. Everything is, quite literally, in a fog; Los Angeles has been enveloped in a low misty haze of water vapor and smog.

My reading habits haven't helped my mood as I've become obsessed with newspapers and they are, as always, filled with bad news. They are particularly focused on "The Crystal Meth Epidemic," which seems only to have become an epidemic now that straight people are dying. As with AIDS, the stories have moved on from the perceived indulgences of gay men to the more sympathetic tales of straight midwesterners gone wrong. Most of the stories feature teenagers in Iowa, Nebraska, Kansas, or some other godforsaken, lonely place, where the rush of obsession and insanity brought on by crystal must be a welcome antidote to the crushing boredom of daily life. I know it would have been when I was growing up there. Those midwestern teenagers have proven to be no stronger than West Hollywood queens. They meet Tina for the first time and find themselves full of chemically induced energy and bravado. The world becomes an enormous, fascinating puzzle for them. Then, without much warning, there comes a night when they wander into a cornfield, lost, running from a nonexistent enemy, and freeze to death mumbling into a cell phone. Or they pick up a gun to express a rage that they never knew existed.

Tired of the shrieking headlines in the newspapers, I decided this morning to read *The New Yorker.* The current issue contains an exhaustive, nearly book-length piece on climate change that did little to improve my outlook on the world. It seems that global warming isn't a steady process. Rather, it builds and builds slowly until one day the accumulated factors create a terrible and irreversible momentum. The story said that the fast, forward momentum has begun. I can feel that momentum inside of me too.

In any case, I haven't been quite right since I've been back from New York. Not working at the House and not writing leaves me with nothing but time, which is always a dangerous situation for me. It's not that I can't go back to the House. I ran into Judy last night in the grocery store and she offered again to take me back.

She was pushing a cart mounded with paper products. Judy has a sixth sense for sales on paper products and, on a hunch, had pulled into the supermarket parking lot on her way home. When she saw me, she patted the heap of toilet paper with satisfaction and exclaimed, "Cheaper than Costco!"

But Judy is nothing if not direct. "Hey you . . . you look like shit," she said after giving me the once over.

I scanned the shelves, trying to seem absorbed by a sale on aluminum foil. "Oh, jet lag. You know."

"Yeah, that jet lag can really get to ya. How was New York?"

"It . . . I came home early." In the face of a two-day trip, I realize how transparent my excuse for leaving the House must be to her.

Judy repositioned some toilet paper in her cart. "Umm-hmm."

"Brought up too many memories."

"That's not always such a bad thing. Just gotta deal with 'em, right?"

Judy's son came hurtling down the aisle at full force and slammed into her cart with a huge bag of tampons. "Look, Mommy, pompoms are on sale!" he shrieked with glee.

Judy picked up her son and covered him with kisses. "That is so great. How did you know I was fresh out of pompoms?"

Her kid stared at her, speaking gravely, "I just knew, Mommy."

I was relieved not to have to talk to Judy further but also knew I was missing an opportunity. With the excuse of her kid being there, I said my good-byes. Judy's always the same. She always keeps the door open. I heard her sharp, chirpy voice as I walked away, "You know where we are!"

There's a good tweaker book study in Silverlake so I head over early to have a walk around the reservoir beforehand. The sun is already fifteen degrees to the horizon as I roar up the incline of Santa Monica Boulevard onto Sunset. The Gauntlet is at the base of the hill, hiding behind a dirty car repair shop. In the daylight, it betrays no hint of the energy that throbs out of it on a Saturday night as leathermen walk quickly, nervously, toward the bar, distrusting the Latino poverty that both disrupts their fantasies and adds a shiver of real fear to their dark, manufactured excitement. On Sunset itself, the Circus of Books looks like the quaint porn bodega it has become. At this time of day there's not much evidence of the sexual flood that washed through the winding streets of Silverlake during its heyday. But it's still here somehow. Regardless of how many sex clubs, bars, and dungeons are ripped out of its flesh, Silverlake will always throb with the sinister, enthralling energy of gay sex.

An ancient leatherman swings around the corner, headed toward Circus of Books. He's wasted by twenty or thirty years of disease but still moving. The seat of his jeans flaps, empty, like an old sack and he's wearing a tank top that was white long, long ago. There's no color to him: hair, skin, and eyes have all gone gray. The sight of his frail, stubborn figure feels like someone has slammed me against the wall and a voice says in my head, "Look." This is The Voice that speaks to me incessantly, whining and needling, accusing me of innumerable crimes and raging against the wrongdoings of others. I remember first hearing it in my teens and thinking of it as a friend, not realizing that it was actually me, or a part of me. It would echo my every thought, repeat every word, and tick off endless lists. As I grew older, The Voice grew louder and louder, less and less friendly. Tireless and smart, it quieted only when its mouth was full of liquor or when feeding on another line of crystal. When I got sober, it was hushed. A few days ago I heard it again. It had been so long absent from my head that I didn't recognize The Voice. I was asleep when I heard it speak, flat and clear. "Liar." I bolted out of the bed thinking someone was in the house. After a few seconds standing in the silent bedroom, my heart pounding, I knew The Voice was back. Now I am used to it once again. My head's ripping slowly down the middle as I keep my eyes locked on the leatherman's bony arm that raises up to push open the door that holds the promise of naked bodies and circling footsteps. But as the old man, who's really probably no more than fifty, disappears inside Circus, I hear The Voice say one more time, "Look."

My car moves to the hills, first plunging down through a

gorge that furrows into the city, digging through oily bedrock. I swing the car alongside the blue of the reservoir and park. Getting out, I don't walk but sit, watching the occasional jogger huff past me. They are mostly women and the place is not nearly as cruisy as it once was. Still, there's something. I sit on a bench and look out to the reservoir in the fading light.

The reservoir becomes the Hudson and I am no longer in Los Angeles but in New York. I thought I could plunge into New York for a moment and then leave it behind. But I've brought it back with me. The memories I wouldn't allow myself in New York wash over me now. Ten years ago I stood in front of the window in my apartment in the Village, looking west. Now I sit in Los Angeles looking back east. In New York, as each night faded to black, I walked in the night, gravitating to the western edge of an island only occasionally recognized as such. Unlike L.A., where the streets are tangled, there is a rigid grid stretching across Manhattan that begins to dissolve only as one moves west through the Village and I walked in that direction every night. Because, on those thin strips of broken concrete that bordered the edge of the island, I felt the water surrounding my little world; water that I only ever saw at night as it blackened and cloaked its true self. In the late hours, its sickly streaked blue was replaced with a dark mystery rasping softly at the city's edges. It was always to those waters that I made my way as the sky darkened. I knew that those waters led to others, shifting around the world, connecting continent to state and frontier to cityscape, pulling at the waste of my life, distilling it into a human constant of degradation. And it is only through scale that degradation attains greatness, only through connecting my poor heart to every other that my personal shame transfigured into something greater.

Looking out over the reservoir, I think I hear waves rustling trash against the side of Manhattan as men circle. Men the world round, circling and waiting to touch one another in dark places, in shaded parks, in back alleys in the Middle East, in front of newspaper walls in China, in public toilets in Germany. They listen to the gurgle of water from fountains, toilets, and pricks as the water goes down, seeking its level. How could I have thought that I was done with this thing? I know very well that I'm not going to the meeting.

Without the protection of a car, Los Angeles reveals itself to be a city again rather than a collection of floating bubbles of private existence. I feel the first little rush of terror knowing that I am out in the city, walking steadily towards men who are available and waiting for whatever I might choose. I need to be on foot tonight to find what I'm looking for, to lose myself in the city without keys, car, or other link to my old life. For so long, I've been hanging on tight, my fingernails digging into my palms, knowing that it's all a lie. Tonight it's different already. I'm not yet prepared to say what I'm looking for but I know. I move quickly away from the reservoir's bit of nature. What I want tonight is crumbling steel buildings, streets as broken as the English spoken on them, and a man who I can see in form but not in face. I want no faces tonight. I don't want to know anything about him, not a name, not even the sound of his voice. I want to know the taste of his chest and the anonymous thrust of his cock. I want to suck on his mouth and fill it before he becomes less of a stranger and his body falls away from me through the familiarity of knowing. Just give me the rush that will come from giving myself to this thing.

I swing onto Rowena Avenue with the goal of another street, Hyperion, ahead of me. Already possibilities present themselves in the cars driving past, containing faces in a prism of colors from white to a cultivated brown to a dark amber and then black. In the dusk, streetlights begin to hum with life. Their light falls heavily on the cheeks of men in passing cars, giving them the chiseled appearance of stone, until they move into another strip of darkness and are lost. Some of their faces stay with me, eyes locked to mine as they travel on long necks, trailing back to me, lingering. Just as they might stop or turn, I break our gaze because what I need tonight can't be done in a car and it can't be done by any of these men. Still, these short connections build my energy. I stride down the street, my boots falling heavily on the concrete.

I travel through a strip of cafés, antique stores, and supermarkets as Rowena rises softly and then drops down onto the roller coaster tracks of Hyperion. Conformity presses in from every side in the form of babies and shopping carts. I try to shut these out before they break the mood. I wish that I had brought along my iPod so that I could further insulate myself. I keep my eyes down until I am on Hyperion. Cars plunge quickly into the small valley. They rush by too fast to notice what goes on in the dark alleys and broken down shacks of houses pushed into the wet mud of the hillsides.

I catch sight of a ragged boy leaning into a car window. He smiles and shifts his weight back onto his heels. I hear a laugh and then he gives a nod and dives into the car, gone. These working boys never sleep but roam continually, fed by Tina, until all the energy of their young bodies drains away. They disappear quickly, as easily forgotten as they are replaceable. When Dino took me to Greece, I was struck by the homemade shrines for those killed on the winding country roads. Those lost people have a memory of themselves left in tin boxes anointed with oil and filled with old wedding photos or a faded Virgin. If we built shrines for all the boys lost on these streets in Silverlake, they would become impassable.

Coming to a steep drive, I remember that it leads to the home of a psychiatrist I once dated. For several years, it seemed that I only dated shrinks. They were drawn to me, perhaps as a challenge. Although I saw him for months, I tried not to speak to him because when I did the fragile illusion of his power was lost. I was met at the door, stripped, and began my work in the entry, pressed down onto gray carpet. Pleasuring him, I was astonished at my revulsion for his old body and how it directly fed my excitement. I was trying to get somewhere during our sessions and I often thought that I was nearly there. On the floor in the kitchen. Locked down on the bed. It worked until he spoke and revealed himself as human. When he allowed the façade to crumble, I began to notice the photos of his grandchildren and the needlepoint pillows on the window seat. Some magic cloak that he had swept around himself was torn away in those moments, leaving only a needy, normal person.

I came to Los Angeles because New York had too many memories. But I realize tonight that L.A. also has history for me. Drunken rampages and tweaked-out rushes of images percolate back up into my mind as I walk down Hyperion. I began coming here on business trips from New York. Those trips were odysseys of blind drunk drives between Santa Monica, where I would stay, and Silverlake. Here are the drawn metal shutters of a now-defunct sex club that I had ended up in one night after a drunken business dinner. Whereas New York had become very tame, L.A. clubs were still unexpectedly extreme. This club in particular, its black walls festooned with slings, had reminded me of the warped intensity of the Mineshaft. But I held back that night too. I wouldn't allow myself to crawl into a sling and let another man take control, shut my eyes, and let it happen. Instead, I got drunker and higher, bottled up my desires and staggered downstairs in the club. I had leaned against a wall, watching, until I felt like I might explode. I don't remember anything about him but a man had approached me. We were kissing, our hands moving over one another, and then he shoved me . . . a nice shove back against the wall. To tell the truth, I enjoyed it. So I shoved back and he seemed to appreciate the antagonistic response rather than me simply giving way. We were like two dogs, sniffing and growling. When he pushed me again, something halfway between sobbing and laughing came from deep inside me. Things moved quickly then as I caught his arm and we turned as if we were waltzing. He was suddenly facing the wall then and, when I shoved again, it was with a force that was not carefully planned but definitely intentional. I hadn't factored in the weakness of the fragile partition that his chest and face slammed against. He went forward and kept moving right through the plywood wall. The men around us froze for a moment and then moved away. There was some blood and no laughing. I was soon standing on the street, this street, ejected but still not satisfied. It still wasn't enough.

I hadn't planned on coming to Cuffs tonight but here it is in front of me, only a few blocks away from the meeting I was planning to attend. "Liar," says The Voice. The building that houses Cuffs is so insubstantial as to be invisible, marked primarily by a black leather curtain covering the open door, breathing in and out, moved by currents of air from inside. The leather stretches out luxuriously, licking at me. I hesitate to really feel this moment because I know very well what it is. I'm not here slumming or even to get laid. I'm here to use. I know it completely. This is what I've been trying so hard to deny. It is why I couldn't work at the House. It's why I couldn't bear to stay in New York. I had to be here, in this moment, and make this decision before I could move on.

I never quite believed it when I heard the old-timers in meetings say, "There'll be a time when there's nothing between you and a drink but God." And here it is. That time. I know that I want to use, but coward that I am, I also want to hedge my bets. Standing on Hyperion Avenue, I say quite audibly, "Please God, keep me safe." The leather curtain on the door draws in, distends again, and then pulls inward with a vacuum that sucks me inside along with it.

Now, in the stomach of the place, I can see almost nothing but a red glow. *Some kinda glorious hell,* I think. The music registers now, reverberating in the tiny space like the inside of a guitar, a song that I've heard many times but it is so distorted and remixed that I can't quite place it. "Lonely boooooooooy." The lyric is buried in a mass of effects that clamor over the words while keeping them ringing ever present in the background. My eyes still adjusting, I take a few tentative steps into the red haze in the direction of where I remember the bar to be. Clouds of scarlet descend from lights over the bar. The ceiling is cluttered with dusty bellows, street signs, and disconnected ductwork. Next to the bar hangs a long S hook, its point glittering dully. I raise my hand and run it down the soft curve of the hook. Caressing the cool vibrating metal of the meat hook, I am not here. I'm back in the meat district with greasy streets flooding back into my mind. I'm in New York crossing asphalt that becomes cobblestone, wandering past limestone that becomes brick. The surfaces are coated with the shiny smell of grease, fat, and sweat as the city proudly lifts its skirts and reveals its filth. I am on Little West Twelfth Street in front of a building posted with warnings of unstable floors and a misspelled epitaph on its front door. "Faggat." Thick chains loop again and again through door handles, loops of metal to keep the devoted away. I am not in Los Angeles but in the rough streets of the meat district looking for the Mineshaft and its rituals of induced insanity. So many times, I stopped in front of the abandoned Mineshaft to smell it and peer through the crack of its chained door into the past. The inky dark preserved memories of a room, a chapel glowing with white porcelain baptismal fonts and Bach organ music mixed with the beat of disco echoing down from above. When I walked Little West Twelfth Street a few days ago in New York, the Mineshaft was gone. The building was not just empty. It had been ripped down. Gone. Or so I thought. But an afterglow still burns inside of me.

"What'll ya have, bud?"

Zooming back. His eyes are almost too blue to exist in the gloom. No shirt, his chest is covered with hair that reminds me of wood grain swirling around his tits and down below his gut. He stares and smiles. "Wanna beer?"

I say something that sounds like, "Unnn."

"Have a beer. On me. Good to see ya." A beer appears in front of me and I stare at it, and then back up at him. Nothing. He brings one of his big furry paws next to my face and I flinch a bit. "Hey. Settle down, little one. Missed you."

"Do I know you?"

He just smiles and turns to wait on another customer who has appeared out of the gloom. My eyes are beginning to penetrate farther into the corners of the tiny space now and I can see white flesh leaning against walls. And then he's back and leaning over the counter to be heard over the music. "Where ya been?"

"Just . . . around, man."

"Still got your room. It's waitin' for ya."

Absorbing the fur-covered forearms, the brush of black forcing out from under his thick arm, I try to summon up

some memory of him in a room. I can imagine but not remember so I just stare into his eyes until I hear myself say,
"Your eyes remind me of mine."

"Always did."

I'm running my hand up the side of the beer. It's cold and
wet in contrast to the bar, which feels hot and humid. I smell
poppers now in the distance. He's happy where he's at, just
smiling, not pushing, but I feel like I need to make an effort.
"So . . . how long's it been?"

"Was wondering myself. Must be . . ." he scratches his gut
and my eyes take in the muscles covered in a soft layer of fat,
" . . . shit . . . almost ten years."

"Yeah. Makes sense. My memory's not so good from back
then . . . if ya know what I mean." I push the beer a little away
from me and smile.

"Don't remember you bein' too fucked up. That's what I
liked so much. That you could do all that so clear."

"Do what?"

"You know." He stretches, displaying his big body, and licks
his lips. "Remember your room now?"

I'm not tempted by the beer. I never even liked beer. Still,
it bothers me that I let it sit there. "Not really. No."

"Hard to believe. Maybe I should show it to you tonight."

"You're workin'."

"Off in a while. You'd like it in there. Where ya belong.
Course it's kinda full now."

"Whatdya mean? Full of what?"

His smile fades and the words fall out of his mouth onto
the counter. "Real full." A dim outline at the far end of the
bar knocks his knuckles on the counter. That big hand again
on my cheek. Rough skin but a soft touch. "No hurry. You're
back now. See what happens."

I search my memory for this man, who certainly seems

like he'd stick in my mind. There were many nights spent in Cuffs when I first moved to Los Angeles but one will always be etched in my memory. It wasn't the end of my using but it was the beginning of the end.

A little more than ten years earlier I'd stumbled past the leather curtain at the door of Cuffs, already drunk and looking for crystal. I was also looking for sex but the two had become so intertwined by that time that it was useless to differentiate between them. The drug made possible the kind of sex I wanted and the sex necessitated the drug.

Cuffs was similar back then except that men actually had sex while standing around the bar and leaning against the back wall. Because I was so drunk early that night and had no crystal, I don't remember much of getting to Cuffs or the men there. The evening starts to come into focus when I think of a bulky guy with a shaved head, probably in his fifties, who leaned against the pinball machine, the lurid colors flashing up at his face. There was nothing attractive about him other than his isolation, his masculinity, and the complete blankness of his eyes. I recall nothing of the conversation that must have preceded our leaving together. Not much remains of the negotiation that always takes place in such a situation. The next thing I remember is him sitting in the passenger seat of my truck, which was still new and fresh, not yet scarred by accidents waiting to happen. He was smoking and I remember that, although it was such a prissy and inconsequential concern, I had never allowed anyone to smoke in the truck. Drunk as I was, I knew that I was betraying something by allowing him to defile the truck's interior. But, by then, he was already in charge.

Next, a flash of pulling up to a bank and him telling me

to get as much money as possible from the ATM. There was no threat or violence. Just a sense that something had shifted in me and that I was engaged in a series of actions that were new and significant. I remember consciously deciding only to get one hundred dollars from the machine and telling him that it wouldn't allow me to withdraw anymore. He was un-concerned, smoking, and assuming that this action would be repeated many times before we were through.

We were in MacArthur Park next, driving along the east side of the park on a street lined by the dark threat of the park on one side and crumbling, bombed out apartment buildings on the other. He had become more animated and nervously told me to park. It was worse when he had taken the money and left the truck, both because I was sure he wouldn't return and because the street was busy with the fast movement of dealers, buyers, and the assorted desperate, all of whom I imagined were staring at the shiny newness of my vehicle. But he did return. Quickly. And he was back in the truck with a rush of stale cigarettes and quiet, stern directions to drive away.

My mind closes from there until I am in his apartment, if it could be called that. I remember it more as a room, perhaps in a boarding house, perhaps in Echo Park. Images rush past my eyes of incredible squalor—clothes and possessions strewn across a floor, a filthy bare mattress with stains that docu-mented its use. The room was bright from a bare bulb and more threatening than if it had been shadowed. There was no escaping the reality of it.

I realized when we were in the room that he was more advanced than I was because sex no longer mattered to him. He was interested only in the drug and sex was nothing more than a distraction. He threw the packets of crystal on the bare mattress and pulled another vial from his pocket. He must have identified it as K because I knew what it was. From under the bed, he pulled a needle, a spoon, a lighter, and some other things I didn't recognize. Not only had I never used needles, I had never seen them used. I tried not to show any sign that I was shocked but I was suddenly very, very sober.

My eyes were locked on the needle like it was a weapon as he filled it and plunged it into the white bulk of his arm. He offered it to me but I mumbled something about snorting and he shrugged. He himself was now snorting the K, having administered the crystal into his veins. I snorted both and waited for the rush. Usually, within seconds, my skull would feel like it was blasting off my head and I would slip into a sexual gear. That night I didn't want sex. I just wanted something painful and intense.

I watched some blood trickle down his arm as he muttered, "Ever since Nam . . . so goddamn mad."

I leaned my head back, feeling the drug dripping down the back of my throat. I said something then that took me past a border into a new world. I remember with absolute clarity asking him, "You wanna let that anger out on me?"

His eyes were so deep and dead they hardly existed. He nodded. "Yeah, man, but we're gonna get more fucked up first."

I don't remember if he shot or snorted more but the amount was impressive. I was still not high. I know that. Everything was completely clear.

I tried to undress him then but he contorted and shoved me away. "Don't . . . fuckin' . . . touch . . . me!"

He started to shuffle around the room then, kicking at the trash on the floor, mumbling, maybe searching for something or perhaps just moving. I stayed still against the wall but started looking at the door. I could no longer understand what he said but he moved faster around the room, flinging filthy clothes against the walls until he stood very still. Frozen. He stared at me as some spit ran out of his mouth.

It seemed like hours that he stood there, breathing heavily and staring at me. Then he fell onto the mattress. He did not lie down, he fell. He wasn't dead because he continued to mumble and scratch at himself, creating long red welts on his white arms and face. I settled down onto the floor and waited. I watched him descend into complete insanity as blood continued to leak from the puncture in his arm. Finally, he jerked himself to the side and just lay there, picking at the mattress.

What I did next was both an act of survival and a fairly clear indication that I was nearly as lost as the man who lay there twitching with paranoia. In one movement, I stood up silently, reached for the remaining drugs, shoved them into my pocket, and was out the door, running. Running.

Much later, in my own bed, the drugs were gone. I had never done K before but it was more powerful than the crystal on that occasion. It had a paralyzing effect—what the boys call a "K hole"—that was like diving into a black hole, sucked along by an unrelenting gravity. While falling faster and faster, I was also completely still. Absolutely certain that I was dying, there was no panic. Only relief.

But once again I didn't die and, ten years later, I'm back at Cuffs. I can see well enough to tell that the place is mostly deserted. It's a weeknight, after all. I walk the circuit of the space. There are probably ten guys positioned around the bar, some sitting on stacked cases of beer, and one standing up above on the little balcony that looks out over the room. Three guys have taken over a corner, talking casually, though their conversation is hidden by the shattering music. They ignore the middle-aged guy who squats on the floor in front of them, rubbing away at their boots, looking up occasionally when one of the men scratches his head like a good dog. I move farther down the same wall so I can see the dog's eyes. They're rolling up in their sockets, full of ecstatic tears. The dog's hands move slowly, intently searching for the spot that will give each man pleasure. One of the guys is wearing shorts and the dog can't resist spending a bit more time on him, working the thick muscled calves, ruffling the fur, and then smoothing it down. His hands dance over the flesh, down to leather boots, and then back to the next waiting man. One of the guys sees me looking, shoots me a smile, and says something. I hold my hand next to my ear and he repeats in a low yell, "Come on, dude. He's always ready for one more." I nod but walk farther down the wall where I can lean back against a railing, under a light focused straight down. There are no mirrors here but I visualize myself, thinking of my body as if it belonged to someone else. I ease my coat off, letting it fall onto a filthy bench. I pull off my shirt, and stuff it into the back of my jeans. I feel too clean for this place. There's no sweaty oil built up on my shoulders. The hair on my chest is orderly, contained within a block starting where my chest rises, and subsiding before my stomach slopes down into my jeans. The light must highlight my cheeks but cast my eyes into shadow. The bartender is staring now, noticing that my shirt has come off and he nods. I stare at him and, for the first time tonight, feel myself start to let go. The distance between us disappears and I'm close to giving way.

I feel the cold beer still in my hand and start to raise it to my mouth just as fingers runs across my stomach and tumble down to fondle my crotch. This one looks like a young pirate, the dark outline of a goatee sculpted perfectly against the smooth skin of his young face. He smiles and looks down at his hand groping against my growing hardness. I just stare.

"Is that a no?" he asks.

"Depends what the question is."

He leans close to me and I can smell strong, cheap cologne. Not what I expected in this setting. I put my beer down. He's not what I want but his smooth tan skin draws my hands up to his chest to feel his pierced nipples. I sense the hardness of surgical stainless steel embedded in rubbery flesh and explore the contrast of hardness and softness while his hands continue to knead me. His eyes narrow as the pressure on his tits increases. His mouth is next to my ear now.

"The question is . . . what can I do to please you?"

His mouth is next to mine now and the roughness of his beard needles at my lip. His tongue tries to work inside me and I want it. He lets some spit bubble out of his mouth and drools it down my chin. When he licks it off, I think of my house and my clean bed and my clean life. My fingers press harder on his nipples and his head pulls back with a gasp.

"Slow, daddy."

"I'm not your daddy."

"No . . . ahhh. Please, man."

"Please what?"

"I don't like pain."

"You're in the wrong place then." His nipples are beginning to feel wet now with something leaking from them and it helps me to rub them harder. His hand jerks away from my crotch and upward to catch my arm.

"Get your fuckin' hand back where it belongs," I growl. And his hand returns to its work as I pull him close to whisper in his ear. "You want me?"

"Ummm."

"Then you're gonna have to give it all up. Just think about yourself like you're somethin' that belongs to me. Somethin' I don't give a shit about. Might put you out in the garage for a while, chain you up 'til I need you. Put you in my living room to put my feet up on while I watch TV. Just fuckin' use you. Cause that's what you want." My thumbs rub hard over the raw tips of the nipples. "Right?"

More pressure and his eyes grow wide, transfixed. I turn him a little to the side so that he can see the dog slave on the floor serving the three guys. They've felt the energy of my scene and are rubbing their crotches, conversation stopped. "See that fuckin' old hag of a slave? That's what you're gonna be when I get done with you. Just use you up and loan you out to my buddies until you don't care what happens, just so somebody with a cock's willing to let you suck 'em." I turn him back to me and now his eyes have a little fear in them.

"I just want you," he whimpers. "Not them."

"Doesn't matter what you want, baby. That's what I'm tryin' to tell you. You wanna please me? My rules. That's what makes me happy. Settin' the rules. If you're gonna come over here and start rubbin' my cock without permission, you better be ready for the whole ride." Little jerks on his tits, "Cause . . . I," punctuating my words, " . . . own . . . you." I pull down hard on his nipples to force him to the floor and I'm not even hard anymore but starting to like it. He struggles so I pull him close. "Get down. Get down, boy. Down on the floor. That's where you're gonna be with me. I'm gonna take you down."

His eyes are wet now and starting to soften. "You gonna hurt me?" He's digging his fingers in the waist of my jeans, trying to get inside. "You gonna hurt me, Sir?"

And I nod and brush my lips over his soft neck and up to his ear. "Yeah. I'm gonna hurt you. Get down now. Get ready."

I let go of his nipples suddenly. The blood rushing back into them makes him gasp in pain and then he moves beyond the pain into that place where all sensations are good so long as they come from me. Some tears now and his chest is starting to heave slowly. My hands are on his shoulders and now he sinks down in front of my crotch. His hands are behind his back, surrendered. The three guys next door are nodding, smiling, and working their cocks. As this man waits on the grimy floor in front of me, I look up and the bartender's gaze is locked on me. He's kinda chewing his bottom lip, swaying back and forth a little bit. The music shifts and a deep voice floats out over the thundering bass, "What we're gonna do right here is go back." The bartender closes and opens his eyes slowly in pleasure. Nods at me. I look down to the floor and the boy has his poppers out, breathing them in deep, his chest thrusting out to make more room for the intoxicant. Smeary dark circles surround his pierced tits. He holds the breath in and then exhales the poison. His eyes are deep black pits and his voice is distorted, "Do whatever the fuck you want to me, Sir. Just hurt me."

Everything around me stops. The music is gone. The only things I can see right now are his eyes and they're like falling down a well. His lips are moving slowly again, repeating a mantra that I can't hear but that I know well enough. "Just hurt me. Just hurt me." My hand draws back, hovering in the air like a conductor with a baton. His lips move slowly. "Hurt me." Tears course down his face, maybe my face too. Suddenly I'm at the door and I feel the heavy leather drape wrap around me, hold me for a second, and then give way to the pressure of my body pushing out. There is cool air on my bare chest and the roar of traffic. I'm out on Hyperion and moving away fast, rushing down the street through a haze of tears but still glancing into the windows of passing cars, looking for a way out. Rising panic, worse and worse, with my head spinning and I stumble, fall, and then just sit there, leaning against a low wall.

The bartender is down beside me, holding me now. He

wraps my leather jacket around me and rubs my face with my shirt. I smell stale beer and poppers mixed in with the sweeter smells of his furry body. I can hear myself sobbing from a distance as he lifts me to my feet and walks me up a street. "Come on," he says and I go because I don't know what else to do anymore.

I'm kissing him in the cluttered living room of a cottage with a rattling floor and a large dog that keeps jumping up on us. "Lola, get the fuck down," he says gruffly and the dog backs off, growling. I want his tongue in me again to fill up my mouth and shut down the barrage of images in my head. I suck on his tongue like it's a cock and he moans, pinning me against the wall and grinding into me.

"You gotta be anywhere tomorrow?" he asks.

"No."

"Wanna get lost a few days?"

"Need to." I'm sort of clawing at him, trying to get him out of his clothes but making no headway.

"Slow down. We'll get there. You need somethin' to help you."

So now this. Presented to me for the first time since I'm sober. In my mind, I whisper, "Please God, no." But with my voice, I ask, "Whatd'ya got?"

"You let me worry about that. You don't got any more choices, little one. Come on. Let's get your room ready."

"My room?"

"Um-hm. Been busy in there but it's still your room."

He leads me down a cramped hallway to the back of the house. The dog is bumping up against us and yelps when he steps on it. He shoves me through the door into the backyard toward a garage. The dog's snarling and he kicks it away. The garage looks dank and cold. Yes, I think. Just right. The door to the garage swings open and he pulls me inside, up against the wall again and kicks the door shut against the dog. Complete blackness and he's in my mouth again, licking out the inside of me.

"Remember your room now, boy?"

"No, Sir. Sorry, Sir."

"Got some friends for you in here. Furry buddies gonna watch while you get worked over."

A scratching and little yelps from behind the door. I pull him closer, feeling inside his jeans for the pounding hardness of him. He's forcing me down now and slapping my face. I turn my face up, anything, just so it doesn't stop.

The scratching again and he rips open the door to stare at the dog, which backs up, barking now. "Lola, back in the house!" He grabs the dog by its collar and pulls it toward the house. I can hear it whimpering as he pulls it away.

The door of the garage swings shut with a bang and I'm again immersed in darkness. There's something comforting about the complete absence of visual markers. I feel like I'm farther and farther adrift. I inch my way into the garage, extending my hands and feeling my way. An edge of a table and something metal. It's cold and, as I pick it up, I feel the sharpness of a blade pushing against my finger. The metal is just dull enough not to cut under the light pressure of my fingers but meant for cutting, meant for slicing through something soft. I try to tell myself that I'm safe with him, that I can take what he's going to do. I met him in a public place, he's got a public job. I let the blade fall to the table and grope farther down. A bottle topples and a blast of chemical harshness. My fingers scrambling trying to pick it up and something soft and, God, it feels like an animal and I recoil, tripping, and falling to the floor.

Looking up, he's standing in the doorway now, washed

with hard white light from a street lamp. At the sight of him, I don't care what I felt on the table. He's everything I need tonight.

"Good boy. Down on the floor where ya belong." He unbuttons his jeans, showing himself to me as I kneel in the darkness and he's still in the light. "Like what you see?"

"Yeah."

"Good boy. And you're gonna remember once we get started. There's no way to forget what I'm gonna do to you." Then he smiles and walks slowly to me. I crouch lower on the floor, waiting. I feel faint, the end is so close.

"Looks like you made a mess. Gonna have to punish you for that." But his voice changes now as he says, "Let's make a little room in here. Ask some of our furry friends if they can move." He hits a light and my eyes blink in the sudden brightness as I try to make sense of the lumps of fur strewn over a long worktable. Above them hang a leather sling and a large wooden X with restraints. He's smiling at me and I'm using every bit of my brain not to understand, to keep the momentum going. But the lumps of fur are all over and then he says, "Been makin' these teddy bears for the last few years. Got a hell of a mail order business goin'." He's holding the thing and stroking it. "Go to the thrift shops and buy old fur coats for nothing. Nobody wants 'em anymore. Good for makin' these little guys, though."

Suddenly the world has righted itself and is pissing down on me. The Voice is howling, "Ooooooh, girl." This apparition of masculinity is suddenly a striving, aging queen doing crafts in his garage. He picks up one of the bears from the sling and coos to it, "You gonna let my friend get in the sling tonight?" He turns to me, holding out the bear, which is dressed in a leather vest with a tiny leather hat on its head. "Cute, huh? Be a good boy and you might get one."

I feel extraordinarily awake and alert now. The dreamy momentum of the night has slipped off me and I'm staring at this guy. I feel too powerful for him. "I don't feel so great, man."

He's by me now and I can't stand him touching me. "What's wrong, baby? Wanna lay down?"

"No, I just . . . it's late. I gotta go. Sorry."

I've turned and I'm out of the garage, headed for the back gate. The dog is snarling at me from inside the house and I hear him calling after me, "Hey! Where you goin'?"

Standing on the other side of the bartender's fence, I can still hear him muttering and shutting up his workshop. My body is covered in sweat and I stink like a bar.

The Voice whispers, *You've already been here.*

My sweat begins to cool in the night air and I lay my cheek against the fence like it's a soft pillow. I feel like my fever has broken. I wait for the Voice to say something else but it's gone.

Chapter 10

BACK TO THE BEGINNING

Whoever said the United States is a beautiful country has never driven from Los Angeles to Iowa during a wet muddy spring. When I received a call from my father telling me that Zelma had only a few weeks to live, I decided immediately to drive to Iowa. I know something about long drives, having driven from New York to Los Angeles a decade ago. What I'd learned on that drive was that the enormity of distance marks well and appropriately the largest of decisions.

I escaped from my "near miss," as I think of it, with my sobriety intact. However, it's clear that I need to decide whether I'm going to recommit myself to being sober or just let the whole thing tumble down. It's one of those decisions that can only be made by driving thousands of miles.

Perversely, I've skipped Las Vegas and the Grand Canyon but have stopped to see "the legendary Black Hills of South Dakota and Wyoming, an oasis of pine-clad mountains on the Great Plains. Home of Mt. Rushmore and Crazy Horse Memorials." When I picked up the tourist brochure for the Black Hills at a truck stop on I-90, I could think of nothing but Zelma's old wedding ring. It seemed destined. So now I stand in front of Mount Rushmore shivering and listening to a tour guide explain, "Each head is as high as a six-story building!"

The tour guide is in her forties and is working a kind of modified mullet peculiar to midwestern women. The modification comes through the addition of a perm, giving the whole "do" the appearance of a Wheaton terrier in need of a bath. Terri, as she tells us repeatedly is her name, has been flirting with me since I arrived and was shuffled into a tour group from the Daughters of the American Revolution. Perhaps she's simply relieved to have someone on the tour under the age of seventy but now I'm thinking that her coquettish manner ("Maybe our visitor from Los Angeles knows when the monument was completed!") indicates that she thinks I might be a romantic interest. I'm a dry tweaker fag on his way to see his dry alcoholic granny, formerly his best friend. We see what we want to see, I guess.

"Aren't they lifelike?" whispers a tough-looking D.A.R. broad next to me. I look around to see if this is addressed to one of her traveling companions. However, they have moved onto the outlook with Terri, who has now taken off her sunglasses and perched them on her head in exactly the same manner I have. Seeing that I'm looking at her, Terri gives me a little smile, mock stamps her foot and motions for me to join the group.

I ignore Terri and focus on the Daughter of the American Revolution. "They're lifelike but . . . they're incredibly sad," I say.

The D.A.R. lady doesn't know what to make of this comment but clearly figures that she started the conversation and has to stick with it. "Now, young man, what on earth would they have to be sad about? They're the Founding Fathers."

"Teddy Roosevelt wasn't a founding father."

Now I've done it. She doesn't like that. Before I was just odd and now I'm a smart ass. "He was a great American. A real patriot. That's what he was."

"My favorite is Abraham Lincoln."

I'm back in her club. In fact, she takes my hand, less in a grandmotherly way than as a confirmation that I've been forgiven for venturing into dangerous territory. "I couldn't agree more." She's smoking now, her lips leaving bright red, waxy streaks on the cigarette's filter. "He saved this country from destruction."

I wonder if the D.A.R lady knows that Abraham Lincoln was gay. I want to tell her that Thomas Jefferson owned slaves and fathered a child with one of them. I want to tell her that I like to snort all kinds of white powders and I haven't been to a meeting in a week. I want to scream and stamp my feet and rip out all my anger by flinging it on top of her. Instead, I hold out my arm and walk her back to the other ladies.

The D.A.R. lady, proud of male companionship, calls out to her fellow patriots, "Look girls! And they say there are no gentlemen left." Terri beams with approval.

Upon leaving the park, a billboard urged me to visit "Cosmopolitan Rushmore Mall, Rapid City. Black Hills Gold! Handcrafted Sioux Beadwork! Star Quilts! Pottery!" The reality of the Rushmore Mall was not so much cosmopolitan as suburban. Still, I could hardly complain once I had eaten two "Rushmore Dogs" with sauerkraut and spotted the display of Black Hills gold in the jewelry store tucked in between Target and Sears.

The ring I bought could be a duplicate of Zelma's wedding ring except that the carving of the grape leaves is more

precise. The ring that I lost was cruder and, therefore, somehow more charming. Though I doubt that the original ring
was hand-wrought, it still had the appearance of something
old-fashioned. One can tell that this ring is one of thousands
pumped out every day by some bland wholesaler. Still, for a
woman near death, it will serve its purpose as a meaningful,
temporary gift.

I finger the ring, flipping it back and forth like a magician, as I drive through the hills of Western Iowa, remembering my geology field trips from high school. Iowa is certainly
not known for hills but those hugging the river are quite dramatic. Not only are they steep, these hills are one of the few
unique landmarks of Iowa. The Loess Hills, pronounced the
Luss Hills, were formed more than a hundred thousand years
ago by fine particles of wind-blown quartz, pulverized by ad-
vancing and retreating glaciers. They are, more or less, enormous sand dunes made permanent.

Compacted by time, the Loess Hills follow the banks of
the Missouri River for miles before giving way to Sioux City.
As a child, Sioux City seemed like an unimaginably glamorous metropolis. Our infrequent trips to the mall there were
exercises in frustration, framed by weeks of anticipation and
the deadly frustration of returning home after only a few hours
of excitement. Though I would not discover it until I was a
senior in high school, Sioux City also had exactly one gay
bar, predictably located near the bus station. Although I can
no longer remember the bar's name, I will never forget the
excitement of parking my car on the deserted city street on a
Saturday night and, shaking with excitement, walking toward
the signless building with a single bare bulb over its front
door. Bars in towns like Sioux City are more than just bars—
they are the entirety of gay life. So when I opened the door,
doubtless looking far too young to be in a bar, no one turned

me away or demanded an ID. In fact, I don't think I even drank in that bar. The excitement of being there was enough. A cowboy with a big handlebar moustache asked me to dance. The song was "I Want a Man With a Slow Hand" and, for the first time in my life, I was in the arms of a man. Later that same night, in a cheap motel on the outskirts of Sioux City, I lost my virginity and got my first case of crabs.

The Loess Hills soon give way to the interminable flatness of Iowa, still mostly gray and wet even though spring has officially begun. The Interstate soon narrows to a flat strip of two-lane highway that zigzags into the center of Iowa. Considering all that it has been through, my vehicle has performed admirably and its cruise control glides me forward, interrupted only occasionally by tiny towns with a single stop light. It takes effort to remember that these towns were once vibrant with fairs and parades and rodeos. Now they are mostly ghost towns with falling down Main Streets surrounded by rings of metal industrial buildings and gas stations. Iowa is in such bad shape that it is considering exempting young people under thirty from state income tax as a lure. However, it's hard to imagine that anyone makes enough money in Iowa that a state income tax exemption would keep them in this godforsaken place.

I dot the time with stops at any roadside diner with a name using a "K" where a "C" should be: Kountry Kitchen, Kozy Korner Café. Kountry Kettle. Grandma's Kumfy Kupboard. These are always promising spots that offer Iowa favorites such as hot beef sandwiches and coconut custard pie. Many require a slight detour from the highway onto an old jumbled street where once grand houses have been converted into apartments or video rental stores, which seem to form most of the retail activity in Iowa. I wonder if I've somehow become a normal person because no one in the Kountry Kitchen gives me a second glance other than to nod at a stranger new to town. Maybe like most of my resentments, my fear of this place is that of a ten-year-old boy, based in the distant, painful past.

Because I make so many stops, it is dark when I near Cherokee. The town sits in a shallow valley and I pull to the side of the road to take it in. From this distance, the town of six thousand could be Los Angeles, its lights flickering in the chill of the spring night. The lips of the valley pucker around the edges of the town, disapproving. The empty fields on either side of the road look desolate and limitless with a rising moon casting a whiteness over them that looks like snow. I turn off the engine and silence sweeps over me. Only the low moans of the truck's settling joints break the constant silence of the night here, and even that small noise seems large enough that I imagine farmers coming to their kitchen windows grumbling, "Past supper! Who's makin' that damn racket?" I remember this silence—so complete that it hums.

As a young man, I would sometimes sit in places like this, alone, swigging cheap vodka from the bottle that was always hidden underneath my seat. On cold, clear nights an Omaha radio station might come in, playing music that seemed like magic to me back when everything was so far off. I'd yearned for those Top Forty hits that I was sure men were listening to while they danced and touched in cities far away. I would strain my eyes on those crystal clear black nights to perhaps see the shining reflections from a distant metropolis, in the blank sky. But only the local towns with strange names like Aurelia, Alta, Paulina, Correctionville, Larrabee, and Moville gave a bit of orange glow to the horizon here and there.

On one of those cold nights, more than twenty years ago,

I'd gone home and picked up the telephone. My parents were asleep so I kept my voice low in the small house. I'd dialed directory assistance for New York City and asked for the number of Studio 54. I don't even know how I'd heard of it. Probably some article in *People Magazine* featuring Liza and Bianca and Andy. I remember the line being busy but I dialed again and again. Each time, the electronic bricks of a magical bridge slipped into place, connecting me to a place that might as well have been imaginary it was so far beyond my grasp. Finally, that night, the call went through and a man's voice shot through the line, barely audible over the pounding beat of the music. "Studio," he'd said. I had gasped, not knowing what to do. "Studio," he yelled one more time. I could not speak but I pressed the phone hard against my ear until I heard the far away receiver slam down, cutting me off.

My parents had stalled their yearly departure for Canada, where they own a fishing camp, thinking that Zelma would die. But she wouldn't or couldn't. My poor mother, tortured by many visits to see Zelma, had advised me to go right before dinner time so as to have an excuse to leave. In heeding this advice, I found myself with a day to fill and no interest in calling long lost high school friends. As sometimes happens in Iowa, the warm spring air had summoned up a kind of bleak beauty with the trees sprouting their first leaves and the brown lawns displaying the first patches of green. I decided to walk without any particular destination in mind.

Iowa is strangely like Los Angeles in that no one walks. The sidewalks, where they exist, are empty and meeting another pedestrian always feels awkward. The difference between Iowa and Los Angeles is that the streets are also largely empty of cars. Only a few vehicles meander past as I wander along the edge of town to a large stand of trees. They are a reminder of when this area was largely forested, before being cleared to serve as farmland. The continued presence of this area, somewhat wild but not nearly a wilderness, is due to the railroad tracks passing through it. Although only a train or two a day now uses the tracks, roads still respectfully keep their distance.

The railroad tracks create a buffer zone well suited to the kind of secret activities enjoyed by children and, as a boy, I spent many afternoons exploring and fantasizing in this area. In the woods I would create traps from branches that were pulled sharply to the ground and fixed in place by a piece of wood that, once stepped upon, released the branch, delivering a vicious slap to the face of an unwitting intruder. I'd also dug shallow pits filled with glass or sharpened twigs that were covered over, probably too crude to fool anyone, but still with the real goal of harming others.

Gay men, like little boys, know how to reach forbidden places and squeeze through the tight openings that block the passage of all but the most determined. As a gay man, I have a special ability to find these places and always feel the lure of woods and abandoned industrial buildings. In cities around the world, as one approaches a park or a wooded area, men begin to appear, their true nature cloaked except to other gay men. Five blocks way from the park, they are businessmen and students, strolling purposefully. Three blocks away, they begin to reveal their intentions with quick looks and a leisurely pace. A block away, the veil begins to slip. A tie is loosened. A few buttons come undone. Upon entering parks around the world, the men no longer have names or occupations or any sense of the continuing business of life. Along the paths, worn by generations of other gay men, they hunt.

I hardly think I'll find sex in these woods, along these trains tracks, but there is still something about being here that makes me vaguely horny and melancholy. I walk past a mound of burned wood where it looks as if someone has made a campfire. Zelma had always told me to avoid the train tracks because the gypsies lived there. She'd always been afraid of them and would sometimes announce, "Hear there's a whole caravan of them gypsies camped outside of town. Lock your doors tonight!" From her ramshackle house, located on the poor side of Cherokee, she could hear the train whistle as it passed through in the middle of the night. She would often say, "Sure is a lonely sound but I like it." After a slug of whiskey, she'd continue, "Where you think all the folks are headed, Pat?"

Aside from the campfire remains, there are other signs of activity along the tracks. I discover mysterious piles of rocks, twigs made into designs, and chalk marks that would make perfect sense to a six-year-old. These appear alongside the rails and, like the train whistle Zelma would listen to, they're lonely but I like them. Further along, a dead bird had been carefully balanced on one of the tracks, supported on either side by pieces of wood to insure the specimen would achieve maximum splatter effect when the next train passed by.

Looking up from the bird, I see a ragged boy beating a tree branch against the train tracks a few hundred feet in the distance. I walk as quietly as possible so as not to alert him to my presence. The branch is a substantial piece of wood and it is difficult to tell whether his objective is to damage the tracks or to break the wood. In mid-swing, the boy catches sight of me and takes a step back, letting the wood thud down onto the train bed. We stare at each other until I'm a few feet away and stop.

"Hi," I say casually, looking down at the piece of wood lying between us. In the morning sun I can see through the boy's yellowish hair to his sweating scalp. It is not the playful sort of hair that one wants to muss and cluck over. The boy carries the sullen look of an unwashed child accustomed to spending too much time alone.

"Hi," the boy says warily. He shows no fear of me even though he must have heard warnings about talking to strangers. But the constant refrains on television about abductions and molestations have not made him timid. Rather, he juts out his chin and moves a little closer to his branch.

"That your bird back there on the tracks?" I ask.

"No," he lies.

"Oh. OK. What are you working on?" I ask, nudging the tree branch with my toe.

The boy steps forward protectively and picks up the branch as if I'm about to steal it. "I'm cleanin' this off."

"Is it dirty?"

"No, the outside. You know, its skin."

"The bark?"

"Yeah, the bark. I'm takin' it off."

The boy has had enough of the inquisition and decides to turn the tables. "What about you? What you doin'?"

"Just walking."

"Where to? Don't got a car?"

"I got a car."

"Then why you walkin'?" he asks.

"I'm going to see my grandmother."

Something about the word grandmother seems to make sense to him so he picks up the branch and begins beating it against the tracks again.

I walk on without saying good-bye but, far down the track,

I can still hear the dull beating of the branch and, if I step onto the tracks, can feel its vibration reverberating through the metal. Far in the distance, I hear a train whistle.

I'm looking at my future, or a possible version of it, in a too hot room in the Cherokee Villa Nursing Center. Spring is in session on the other side of a double paned window but here the world is without time or seasons. There is a constant rattle from nurses, wheelchairs, and med trays—the equipment of death. There is another rattle, or perhaps a wheeze, coming from Zelma. I recognize it. Not that I'm a great expert on death but I've heard this breath before. It is deceptively quiet but has the ability to fill a room because each round of inhalation and exhalation is numbered. That same breath counted down Dino's last days in New York.

Although she would sometimes say that she "had the blues," Zelma was more manic than depressive. She never took to her bed in the middle of the day, preferring the perch of a chair where she could doze, observe, and reach for her lined writing pad when something floated up out of the past. Today, however, she is curled up on top of a crocheted blanket, fully dressed, shrunken like a discarded little puppet. She doesn't look like she's dying, just like she's sleeping.

It's unfair that I've come here without telling her but my parents couldn't bear the monologue that would have started had they told her before they left. "Oh, I worry about him on those damn airplanes." Airplanes have replaced trains in her imagination so she would have looked wistfully out the window and sighed, "I see the little white tails of those jets goin' by and I wonder where all those people are headed. Just makes me lonesome." Something reassuring would have been

offered about the safety of air travel to which she would have
replied, again and again, "Oh, those damn planes. Why does
he have to fly?"

So, instead, I stand here watching this thin brittle thing
that was my grandmother and wonder whether she will, quite
literally, have a heart attack when she sees me. Four years, five
years. How long has it been?

I sit on the edge of the her bed, put my hand on her bony
shoulder, and say softly, "Grandma. Grandma, wake up."

She opens her eyes. They are a startling shade of light
blue, intensely focused but looking elsewhere. She stares at
me. Am I another nurse come to poke her or try to persuade
her to bathe?

I brush her face with my hand, "It's Patrick, Grandma."

Now a kind of scrambling, pulling her bony limbs around,
trying to go somewhere and then just laying still, looking at
me until her voice emerges, still loud enough to pierce any
wall. "Paaaat? I never thought I'd see you again."

I help her out of the bed and into her chair. As she gets
up, an unwashed old lady smell wafts off her. "Why, Pat? What
on earth . . . ?"

"I came to see you."

And now she sits. Not smiling but taking it in. She picks
at her blouse, pink roses on a light blue field, dotted with assorted stains. She is content, somewhere between here and
there. Then the world rushes back to her, her head cocks and
that choking voice trills again, "Why Paaaat, what on earth?"

"I wanted to see you."

"Well, God bless you dear."

Zelma picks up a disheveled box of Russell Stover choco-
lates and rummages around in it. Warily extracting a bonbon,
she shoves her thumb into the underside and peers at the fill-
ing. With a look of disgust, she plops it back in the box.

"I just don't want to eat no more."

"Do you feel sick to your stomach?"

"Noooo. Just don't wanna eat."

"You should eat. You'll get weak if you don't eat."

She's somewhere out the window, her eyes following something I can't see but now she's back on me, "Why Pat, I thought I'd never see you again."

I've been here for less than a minute and I want to rush out the door. There is another lady, comatose, in the room. She is a tiny pile of bones huddled in the middle of her bed.

"Do you talk with your roommate?"

Zelma's voice is, if anything, louder, "Heck, no. She's ignorant."

"Oh."

"I wish I could get a roommate with some brains."

"She looks like she's sick."

"She don't got no brains. Ignorant." Zelma's eyes are extraordinarily blue. Bluer than I remember. Focused but crazy. She fixes me with them now. "You know what I'd give my left arm for?"

"What Grandma?"

"A good cold beer."

"I guess that's not allowed here. You know I don't drink anymore. I'm an alcoholic."

"Vodka was my friend," Zelma says before she retreats, her eyes focused far away.

I reach into my pocket, thankful for the diversion of a gift. "Grandma, remember I told you that I lost your Black Hills gold ring?"

"Oh, heck, that don't matter, Pat."

"Well, it mattered to me and I'm really sorry." I draw out the ring and Zelma's eyes follow its dull sparkle. "I bought this for you in the Black Hills."

Zelma reaches for the ring reflexively and takes it close to her face, examining it, fingering the round coolness of it. She tentatively pokes her long bony ring finger into it, sliding the ring nearly down to the knuckle before pausing.

"Well, Paaat, I don't need no more rings."

"I know you don't need one but I wanted you to . . ."

"No." This is not a shy protest or even a petulant one. Zelma's voice is flat. She pulls the ring back off her finger. "You keep it, Pat. I don't need no more rings where I'm goin'."

Zelma's eyes never leave mine as she takes hold of my hand and slides the ring onto my finger. I'm surprised at the steadiness of her grip. She stares at my hand and then pulls it to her face for a moment. This feels almost unbearable. I want to pull away but, instead, I stand there with my face burning red until a plump young nurse pops her head into the room and announces dinner. Zelma drops my hand without further comment, shuffles around underneath her blanket as if to get up, but then settles back down into her chair. She lays still for a few breaths and then turns her head to look out the window. "They feed us pretty good here at the Villa."

"Good. You should try to eat something."

"Food ain't got no flavor. No salt."

"Here. Let me help you get up, Grandma."

It seems odd to me that someone who is supposed to be near to death is asked to go to the dining room to eat but the nurse had told me, "We like to keep her moving. She's quite a handful otherwise."

We shuffle down the hallway together and into the dining room. Zelma seems to have a number of old men who are admirers and each of them greets her. She sails past them, without a word, to an empty table. Positioning herself at the table, across the room from the old men, she announces loudly, "This is my grandson. From California."

They all nod at me and Zelma trills out again, "The writer. From California."

Suddenly, I have to go and there's no way to say anything but, "I love you, Grandma," before the tears start to come.

She wraps her old bony arms around me and the years slip away as she says, "And I love you. You never forget. You're a good person, Pat."

Zelma died that night. Without warning or hospitals, she left. I'd said about all I had to say to her and I'm glad for that. Yet, there is this ache of knowing that she had waited for me before she died. I reran all the years that went by when our relationship was reduced to a series of Hallmark cards infrequently spaced throughout the year and a desultory phone call at Christmas. I've sat in enough Twelve-Step meetings to see that we both played a part in our estrangement. Still, I cry with regret as I turn the cool ring of Black Hills gold around my finger like I'm winding it, feeling not the ring but Zelma's touch.

Driving back into Los Angeles, nothing feels real. Especially this city. I don't understand how I got here.

In the late afternoon I glide past slowly bending oil wells, losing myself in the hazy light of Los Angeles. I'm like something injected into the bloodstream of the city. Foreign. Focus, I think. See this place. But it is impossible to see Los Angeles up close. Every mini-mall is a city onto itself. To keep myself from driving off the road, I force myself to register the Arab chicken joint and the special price for laundered shirts on hangers at a dry cleaner. *Should check that out*, I tell myself, feeling somehow useful. But I won't because I've developed this fear of blocked parking lots and left turns that seem to break the flow of things. I'm moving too fast to stop. The way to see L.A. is not in the details but in the long view. From here, for example, where the road hovers high above the basin. From here, the city promises everything it promised the first time I saw it.

The drama of the Santa Ana winds makes it even lovelier. In the middle distance, lines of towering palm trees whip back and forth over the oasis of the city, hugging the green water-soaked environs of Beverly Hills. The trees, slyly prehistoric things, twist in the wind, alive. The Hollywood Hills loom over the city, so immediate that their towering mass seems in danger of collapsing. The light in California is unique, strongly angled and diffused through the particulate matter in the air, making objects appear unreal, and their distance uncertain. When the winds rise over the desert portions of the state, they do not clear the air but suspend a grainy dust that further obscures the hard lines of manmade structures, favoring instead the always-present outlines of mountains and trees. In the bleakest industrial landscape in California, I've often lost myself in a reverie of nature elicited by the howling desert air.

It really is as if a fever has broken in me and I am so tired. I just want to go home and sleep. But there's something that must be done first. If I don't do it now, it will mean less to me later. So I reach over and touch Zelma for a moment. "Is it OK?"

I've been sitting on the ridge of a mountain in Griffith Park for nearly an hour, waiting for night to come. The park closes at dusk and it will be difficult to find my way back to the road in the darkness but Zelma has never seen the lights of the city and I want to show them to her. I reach down and pick up the little cardboard box that contains the ground bits of my grandmother and hold it close to me. I also have the dirty little blanket from her bed and I pull it around us against the cold of the Los Angeles night.

The lights of the city are beginning to flicker down below like fireflies. They gather and surround us from our position on the ridge, perched between the expanse of the San Fernando Valley, the abrupt spires of downtown, and the sweep of the L.A. basin down to the sea. Stars are not visible through the cloak of smog but a huge yellow moon has appeared out over the desert.

Zelma wanted to be sprinkled in the Rocky Mountains. For someone whose life was such a headlong rush to nothing, she had thought about her death very clearly. I remember her regularly announcing when I was a child that she had already paid for her cremation because she didn't want to be a burden. She had been planning her death for fifty years. She wanted no funeral, only to be sprinkled in the Rockies. Whether she had just seen the Rockies in the distance when visiting my uncle in Denver or had actually driven into the mountains with one of her husbands, I have no idea. She may have just summoned the Rockies from her brain or an old issue of *Ideals Magazine*. But, whatever her source, she had painted them many times. In Zelma's paintings, the mountains were always distant and silhouetted. She wanted the dramatic outline without the distractions of trees, roads, and people.

A few days ago, my father and I stood in the Rocky Mountain National Park with this same box of Zelma. As my mother stood guard against rangers who might witness our illegal activity, we poured Zelma out into the wind over a valley that contained a meandering creek, lonely pine trees, and blue outlines of ragged mountains in the distance. It could have been one of her paintings. My Dad didn't cry because he doesn't and I didn't cry because I already had but he held me close to him afterward and I knew that I'd done something for him that only I could do. It was, as they say, a gift of sobriety.

But I'd kept a little bit of Zelma to add to the gritty cloud floating over Los Angeles because, in the end, this really is my home. For all of its strangeness and frustration, I know that I will always be here in L.A. Like so many other disaffected and desperate New Yorkers, I had come here a decade ago because I'd run out of options. I still feel that way sometimes but I'm not willing to run anymore. I know I have to stay and face this thing inside of me. So if I'm to be here, I want a little bit of Zelma floating around me, catching in my throat, and lodging herself in my eye from time to time.

It is so cold in L.A. at night. I pull Zelma's blanket closer around me. My mother laundered Zelma's blanket and although its smeared chocolate stains and magic marker streaks will always remain, it smells of nothing but Tide detergent now. On a corner of it, Zelma had written her name, as if someone might steal this last little thing that she had all to herself.

The carpet of light spreads out around me in all directions now, only a rim of indigo remaining above the horizon. At this moment, in this physical setting, Los Angeles is the most wondrous place on earth. It is clearly time so I open up the box that still contains a substantial layer of Zelma dust. There is no wind, not even a breeze, so to shift her into the air out over the cliff will not work.

Instead, I look straight up to where I know there are stars I cannot see. I look right up into the yellow glare of the rising moon and, box and all, I throw Zelma as high as I can into the sky. I throw her to another place. I throw away her pain and try to add mine to it. As the box tumbles and spins in the air, a fine layer of Zelma drifts down on me.

I love you and I won't forget you. I'll try to understand and to connect. In memory of you, I'll try again to be happy.

Please help me.